HONG KONG MANAGEMENT CASES IN INFORMATION SYSTEMS MANAGEMENT

HONG KONG MANAGEMENT CASES IN INFORMATION SYSTEMS MANAGEMENT

Compiled and edited by

The Management Development Centre of Hong Kong

The Chinese University Press

The Management Development Centre of Hong Kong

ISBN 962–201–756–8

The Chinese University Press
The Chinese University of Hong Kong
Sha Tin, New Territories
Hong Kong
Fax: +852 2603 6692
E-mail: cup@cuhk.edu.hk
Web-site: http://www.cuhk.edu.hk/cupress/w1.htm

Printed in Hong Kong

Contents

Preface

Realizing that there is a shortage of locally relevant management cases which could be used by trainers and teachers in Hong Kong, the Management Development Centre started to change this situation in 1987 by publishing the first English language edition of the case compendium in early 1989. Since then, three other case compendia have been published. The compendia have been widely used by various educational institutions which teach management in the territory. They are also proving useful to many of the training providers in Hong Kong, and to many companies using cases for in-company management training.

In order that management trainers can use the cases more effectively, in collaboration with The Chinese University Press, a series of Hong Kong case books which trainers can use in a classroom environment, will be published starting from 1996. Again, all the cases included in the series are local ones. They can form the core of a teaching or training session for a group and, of course, as projects or exercises to identify development needs.

We acknowledge the commitment and hard work of the many authors of these cases and those who carried out the technical review and editing of this case book.

The Management Development Centre
of Hong Kong
September 1996

Acknowledgements

We would like to acknowledge the special effort made by Mrs. Eva Wong from the Department of Information Systems at the City University of Hong Kong. She has helped us with the publication of this book by gathering relevant materials and coordinating the writing of some of the cases, as well as reviewing them. We would also like to acknowledge contributions from her colleagues in the same department.

The cases in this book are drawn from a number of sources and any resemblance to existing companies is coincidental.

Introduction

What is a "case study"? It is a representation of reality. Usually, it is a problem taken from real life. Indeed, all of the cases in this book are based upon events that actually happened in Hong Kong.

Each case should contain sufficient background data for students to identify the issues and put forward proposed solutions. No case can, by its very nature, contain all the information needed for a perfect decision. However, that is itself like the world in which the practising manager has to live. Most managers operate in conditions of incomplete knowledge and can never be sure about the impact of their decisions. Moreover, decisions seldom prove to be "right" or "wrong." The situation that a manager faces is seldom that clear-cut.

Tackling a Case

If you are a student faced with a case study for the first time, this may look a pretty daunting task. You may be at a loss to know where to start. The guidelines below are by no means comprehensive but you should find them useful.

Step 1: Groundwork

Read the case through quickly to give yourself an idea of the "big picture." Re-read the case, marking what you consider to be the key areas or the areas about which you are uncertain.

Step 2: Problems

After a third reading, list down what you see as the main problem areas. Prioritize these problems:

1. Which are the most important?
2. Which are having the biggest impact and why?
3. Which demand the most immediate attention and why?

Step 3: Analysis

1. How did the problems occur? What are the causes?
2. Do not fall into the trap of confusing symptoms with core problems.
3. Where you do not have sufficient information, make assumptions that you can rationally defend.
4. Most fundamentally, are all these problems actually capable of solution?

Step 4: Alternatives

Most problems can be tackled and "solved" in a number of different ways. Generate possible courses of action and test them by asking yourself:

1. How many of the problems will this solve?
2. To what extent will they be solved?
3. Will this solve the most important, most basic problem(s)?
4. What resources will this course of action require? Are they available?
5. Are there any disadvantages to this solution? What are the risks?

Step 5: Action

Which course of action is the "best"? Be sure that you are explicit about what makes it "best." Is it speed, economy, acceptability?

   Draw up your plan answering these questions:

1. *What* is going to be done?
2. *Who* is going to do it?
3. *When* is it going to be done and what are the stages along the way?
4. *How* is it going to be done? Set down the detail of your approach.
5. *Why* is it going to be done that way?

   If you follow these steps and can answer these questions, you are probably well on the way to an effective case solution.

Step 6: Confirmation

A useful check, when you have completed your work on the case, is to go through the following process.

Findings	Conclusions	Recommendations
1. 2. 3. 4. 5. 6. 7. 8.	1. 2. 3. 4. 5.	1. 2. 3.

1. List your findings, the information that you have gathered about the situation described in the case.
2. Write down your conclusions based on your findings. Each conclusion *must* be based on your findings. You cannot make conclusions that are not backed up by *facts*.
3. Draft your recommendations for action. Every one of your recommendations *has to be* supported by at least one of your conclusions.

In the diagram, Recommendation 1 is backed by Conclusion 1. However, Conclusion 1 is not based on findings. Hence, it is not being supported.

Part I

Human Issues

1

How to Make People Work Together?

Eva Y. W. Wong

The University of Causeway had a staff problem. It was difficult to tell whether the University was short of staff or had too many because no one knew exactly how many people were officially employed by the University.

Three departments were responsible for staffing matters, and the correct staff number should be available. Personnel Office had a set of staff records which were carefully maintained using a networked computer system worth of $200,000. Payroll Section ran its weekly and monthly payroll accounts on a minicomputer worth of $250,000 purchased for administrative sections. Management Accounting Section, which was responsible for planning and budgeting for the University, held a staff database on a microcomputer worth of $20,000. Each section held and maintained its own records on its own system. Reconciliations were never done, discrepancies were never resolved, their figures never agreed. As a result, the Vice-Chancellor did not have information to make the decision to hire or fire people because he was not sure whether a department was understaffed or overstaffed. Furthermore, the planned annual budget got thrown out by the Financial Board meeting because the staffing figures were unsound.

This was the reason why the Management Information System (MIS) Section was called in to help. It was charged with the task of reconciling the Personnel and Payroll systems, thus providing exact staffing figures for Management Accounting to plan the budget for the University.

The first problem to tackle was to form a work team consisting of personnel in the three sections. It might be the organizational culture at Causeway, or just plain human characteristics, that people in the three sections simply did not have faith in the others. They were dedicated to their own jobs, sceptical of the others and very protective of their own systems. Each section perceived that its system was the best one, and that it was faultless. Each system seemingly gave its section authority, position and an image of being technologically advanced. People in each section would not want to know how the other systems functioned and they certainly would not allow others to even try to understand theirs. The idea of cooperating the three sections was very difficult to be accepted because this meant revealing their systems for all to see, learn, use, and criticize. They were worried that this might lead to changes of systems, alterations of working practices, or even loss or gain of job definitions. Besides, questions such as "Why should I change my system to accommodate theirs?" and "Why should I be the one lumbered with all the work?" lingered in everyone's mind.

PERSONNEL   PAYROLL   ACCOUNTING

The MIS Section must coordinate in such a way that staff in the three departments involved would put aside their pride, prejudices and fears to communicate with each other. Most important of all, they must learn to trust one another so that they could work together to deal with the problem in hand.

Questions for Discussion

1. What can MIS Section do to help the three sections learn to trust each other and achieve cooperation?
2. How can this problem be avoided in future?
3. Would the present trend to boundaryless organization be applicable in a university?

2

Expanding an Airline and Maintaining Profitability

Robert Davison

Hong Kong-based airline Flying Tiger has successfully tapped a local market in high-quality service provision for the China market, as well as some regional destinations. Currently it flies to thirteen destinations in China, seven in Southeast Asia and Japan, and various other charter destinations. In the near future, it expects to take over from Air Taiwan some routes to Taiwan. Its employees are primarily from the Southeast Asia region, some "borrowed" from Air Taiwan with whom it shares maintenance and other facilities.

Flying Tiger also has one of the most modern and economical fleets in the world with seven A320 airbuses (seating approximately 150 passengers each) and three A330 airbuses (seating approximately 300 passengers each). While its seat prices are typically higher than those of its competitors — China-based airlines and regional airlines in other countries, all its flights are fully booked well in advance. Clearly it has established a profitable and identifiable niche market. The challenge for Flying Tiger is to expand and yet to maintain the current competitive advantage. Clearly the next century will see a great deal of competition in the air travel market, as new entrants particularly from China enter the market-place so as to capitalize on the rising number of regional travellers.

Question for Discussion

Using an information systems perspective, as well as with reference to appropriate models of competition and growth, explain how information systems can be utilized in order to help Flying Tiger to expand.

You should focus on both of the following two areas:

1. Human resources management in Flying Tiger.
2. Marketing and advertising of the Flying Tiger product.

In each area, you should identify the key questions which need to be addressed. You should also point out which issues are important and how those issues can be tackled with information systems.

Part II

Changes in Organization

3

Information Systems — Can It Help the Ming Wai Corporation?

Eva Y. W. Wong

Eating is big business in Hong Kong. This is especially true for Ming Wai Corporation which has twenty Chinese restaurants at various locations in the territory.

Each restaurant serves dim sum from 6:00 a.m. in the morning and dinners from 6:00 p.m. in the evening. On top of these, banquets which begin at 3:00 p.m. in the afternoon with *mahjong* games and finish at 11:00 p.m. at night give the best profit margin.

Chris Chow inherited the business from his parents five years ago. Chris's major headache about the corporation is the amount of food and drink inventories that have to be stocked to keep the restaurants in operation. Food items are perishable. Seafood, in particular, was to be alive and fresh before being consumed. Hence it is not a good management practice to keep large quantities of food. Yet the risk of insufficient food stock is just too high for the corporation to bear. If one of the restaurants ran out of food, especially during a banquet evening, it could severely damage the good name of the corporation and could also lead to loss of future business. Compounding this problem of food inventory is that of drink. Drink stock is much more expensive than food. The consumption of beverages, both alcoholic and soft, is negligible during the day compared with evening meals. Drink gives a much higher profit margin than food, and they do not rot, hence it is essential that drink is stocked up when prices are low.

At present, each restaurant keeps its own inventories of food and drink, and works out its own reordering schedule. There is no correlation or cross-referencing between restaurants. As a result, restaurants in popular locations usually have an out-of-stock problem, whereas others in less favourable places have stagnant stocks. Since a considerable amount of the group's expenditure is on food and drink stocks, and the corporation's major revenue comes from the restaurant business, Chris has to come up with a specific strategy to deal with this problem.

One possible way is to have a department set up for central purchasing. This department will then be able to look at the supply and demand of food and drink of each restaurant and regulate inventory levels for the whole group. To do this, however, means that each branch manager will have to prepare detailed stock level reports of the restaurant on a more frequent basis than the current practice of once every six months. Furthermore, analysis of the data and information represents another huge task to surmount.

Another area of concern is personnel. The corporation employs in excess of 5,000 people, ranging from branch managers to general waiting staff. There is a shortage of people at all levels. In the good old days, a family member could stand in as manager, cook, waiter or as anything that was required. Now, Chris cannot ask his son to stand in as a waiter even for an hour! Employing foreign workers is not an avenue open to the group as Cantonese is almost a must in the restaurant business.

One way he perceived that could help the situation is to have staff mobility. That is, calling in staff from less busy restaurants to help out at busy ones. To do this would require the banquet appointments of all the restaurants and the working schedules of all the staff in such a way that mix and match can be compiled. Personnel takes the lion share of the group's expenditure. Careful management of these people to ensure that they will stay with the corporation and work effectively and efficiently for the benefit of the corporation is of paramount importance.

Chris was sitting in his office, contemplating what to do, or more precisely, what could be done, when an advertisement in the *South China Morning Post* caught his attention. It read, "Information Systems — The Application of Information Technology to Cope with Business Problems." "Is this the solution?" he asked himself.

Questions for Discussion

1. How can information systems be employed to help:
   a. to keep food and drink inventories at optimal levels?
   b. to manage personnel so that staff mobility and interchange-ability can be achieved?
2. What kind of new problems may the corporation encounter with the implementation of information systems?
3. The Chinese restaurant is a traditional business. Is information technology appropriate for its environment?

4

Poly-Bank Corporation

K.T.B. Siu

Summary

In January 1995, Poly-Bank Corporation, a U.K.-owned bank, relocated its headquarters to Hong Kong. This resulted from Sir Y. Y. Jacobson's (Chairman of Hong Kong General Chamber of Mining Industries) decision to diversify 20% of his US$95 billion investment from his international oil mining business to Poly-Bank Corporation in Hong Kong. This was an attempt to position the bank towards a better share of the banking market in Hong Kong and Southeast Asia.

Poly-Bank planned to move to the forefront of information technology usage to support its banking information systems products and services. The Group Information Services (GIS) department of Poly-Bank was expanded from a staff of 80 in January 1995 to staff of 280 in June 1996. The Senior Manager of GIS, who was recruited by Poly-Bank through PERT International Management Consultancy Firm in July 1995, left the bank in June 1996 to emigrate to Australia.

As Senior Manager of Retail Banking Services, you worked closely with the Senior Manager of GIS during the last year on the specification and implementation of a PATELL (Poly-Bank Automatic Teller machine) system to support Poly-Bank's 500 branches. In July 1996, you were asked by the Group Staff Controller and General Manager of Poly-Bank to take up a newly created position of Chief Information Officer and Assistant General Manager of GIS.

Poly-Bank Moves into the Forefront of Information Technology

Background

Poly-Bank Corporation invited Sir Y. Y. Jacobson onto its Board of Directors in January 1995 after Sir Y. Y. decided to invest in the Poly-Bank. At the Board Meeting in January 1995, Sir Y. Y. indicated to the Chairman that he was supportive of the bank's move to the forefront of information technology usage to support its information systems products and services. Because of this, the bank will be able to get ahead of Mono-Bank Corporation (which was monopolizing the banking business in Hong Kong) in five years' time. As a result, a budget of HK$72 million per year and a hardware/software budget of HK$120 million (over a period of three years) were allocated to the GIS department of Poly-Bank Corporation in March 1995.

The strategic objective of Poly-Bank's investment in information technology was: "To be ahead of Mono-Bank in five years' time by using advanced information technology products to build sophisticated banking information systems products and services."

In July 1996, Poly-Bank Corporation had an organizational chart as shown in Figure 1.

Manpower

In January 1995, Poly-Bank's GIS had a Manager with 79 staff as shown in Table 1.

In July 1996, GIS had an organizational chart as shown in Figure 2.

Hardware

In January 1995, Poly-Bank had two minicomputers supporting the bank's current accounts, documentary credits, fixed deposits, foreign exchange, import/export, loans, and savings accounts systems.

In March 1995, following the Board's decision on the allocation of hardware/software budget, GIS had undertaken the projects below:

1. An IBM RS/6000 was ordered in March 1995 for delivery in

Figure 1: Organizational Chart of Poly-Bank Corporation, July 1996

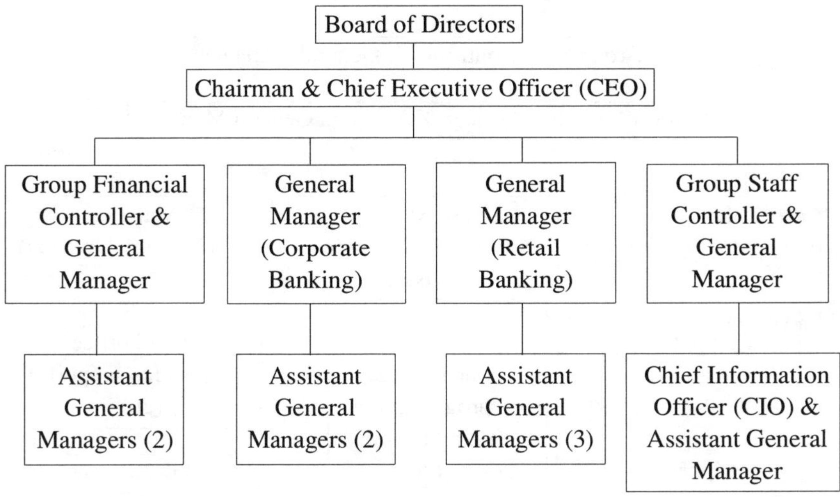

Note: Number in brackets represent number of staff.

Table 1: Number of Staff in Group Information Services Department

Project	Systems analyst	Analysts/Programmers
Current accounts	2	15
Documentary credits	1	3
Fixed deposits	1	4
Foreign exchange	1	7
Import/Export	1	9
Loans	1	3
Savings accounts	3	28

January 1996. Conversion to the IBM hardware required the associated changes in:

a. operating system,

b. change-over to IBM programmer terminals,

c. installation of IBM communications controllers.

Besides hardware changes, a conversion project of the savings accounts and current accounts systems to the IBM hardware was carried out in 1996.

Figure 2: Organizational Chart of Group Information Services Department, July 1996

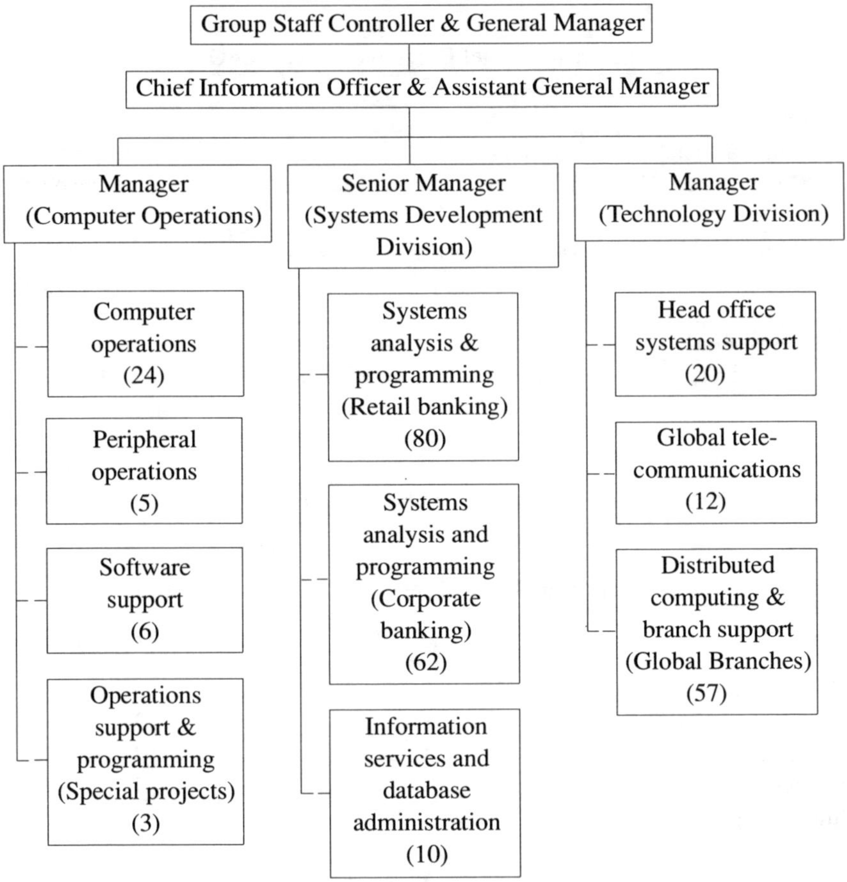

Group Staff Controller & General Manager

Chief Information Officer & Assistant General Manager

Manager (Computer Operations)	Senior Manager (Systems Development Division)	Manager (Technology Division)
Computer operations (24)	Systems analysis & programming (Retail banking) (80)	Head office systems support (20)
Peripheral operations (5)	Systems analysis and programming (Corporate banking) (62)	Global tele-communications (12)
Software support (6)	Information services and database administration (10)	Distributed computing & branch support (Global Branches) (57)
Operations support & programming (Special projects) (3)		

Note: Number in brackets represent number of staff.

2. The two VAX 6220s which were running the SWIFT messages were planned to be upgraded by October 1996 based on annual growth rate. No changes were made to the terminals which were used for sending and receiving messages.

3. On the personal computer side, 80 IBM PCs were planned for delivery in March 1996 to a group of Senior Banking Officers for the following functions:

    a. Spreadsheet analysis for budgeting;

    b. Download of data from the IBM mainframe to the IBM PCs for spreadsheet analysis on market trends of:
- interest rates,
- exchange rates.

4. Poly-Bank also planned the following projects to be implemented after installation of the PCs:

    a. Use of the PCs for the bank's Marketing Officers to check customers' information and their account balances;

    b. Development of decision support systems for use by the bank's Senior Banking Officers;

    c. Development of an investment planning prototype for bankers to decide on the acquisition of small banks in Hong Kong in order to take over their share of the banking market;

    d. Development of an expert system to enable the credit card department to allocate credit limits to credit card applicants.

Software Plan

The IBM MVS operating system was planned to support the following facilities:

1. 300 simultaneous users working on online compilation and testing of programs.

2. Development environment of the Time Sharing Option systems supporting:

    a. clients and/or server operations;

    b. interactive programming facility for program development;

    c. DASD access.

For database management systems software, Software AG's Adabas and Cullinet's IDMS/R Relational Database Management System were being considered for the bank's new Multi-Currency Savings Accounts project, in addition to IBM's DB2 Relational Database Management System. Problems with DB2 was that there had been no banking or airline users who could give comments on its performance.

Network Decisions

Poly-Bank had been using public network software, and the Datapak service from the local telephone company since 1985. The idea for a private data network had been proposed by Poly-Bank's Assistant General Manager of Group Finance in July 1995 on a cost-saving basis. Owing to Poly-Bank's limited exposure to the telecommunications field, the decision on private data networks could not be made in September 1995. In addition, the list of systems application development projects seemed to occupy all the planned manpower for the following two years.

Despite GIS's recommendation, the Assistant General Manager of Group Finance had written a memorandum to the Group Staff Controller requesting to raise the priority of developing a Poly-Bank's private integrated data network which should cover voice, data, and image for Poly-Bank's long-term reduction in communications costs.

The Banking Industry in Hong Kong

Monopolized by Mono-Bank since 1980

Mono-Bank Corporation, with its current dominance in Hong Kong, first started its business in 1875 as a money exchange house. It later developed into the banking business and expanded its operations by taking over a number of small banks in the period 1950 to 1970. As of 1996, Mono-Bank had 480 branches in Hong Kong and 280 overseas offices around the world.

Over 55% of Hong Kong's companies made use of Mono-Bank's autopay system for salary payment to their employees. This facility, together with Mono-Bank's network of 800 electronic banking terminals, had attracted over three million savings accounts customers.

Poly-Bank Entered the Retail Banking Market in 1996

During the period July 1995 to December 1996, Poly-Bank increased the number of its branches from 130 to 500. On an average, it took only fourteen minutes for a new customer to complete the opening of a savings account. Once opened, a customer could obtain cash advances of up to two months' salary. By the end of March 1996, Poly-Bank had completed installation of all its 1,000 PATELL terminals outside its 500 branches.

As at the end of June 1996, Poly-Bank had a total of 1.8 million savings accounts customers.

The Information Systems Backlog and the Information Technology Opportunities

Poly-Bank's Information Systems Backlog

In January 1995, Poly-Bank's senior management had identified the following banking information systems products to be developed in the following three years:

1. A Poly-Bank Automated Savings Account System which should cover the bread-and-butter type of transaction-oriented fast-processing system with:
    a. multiple-currency savings,
    b. signature verification by a new banking terminals with local intelligence.
2. A Poly-Bank Automated Corporate Customer Terminal System which would enable Poly-Bank's corporate customers to install personal computers within their companies for direct debit and credit transactions on their own accounts.
3. Poly-Bank's own version of cheque clearing system called Poly-Bank Automatic Cheque Handling and Transmission System which can reduce the cost that were charged by Mono-Bank to execute the cheque handling and clearing operations for Poly-Bank.
4. A front-office Treasury Trading System which should allow the Treasury Traders to operate on a touch-screen type workstation for connection to an AS 400-based back-office system. (This would run the MIDAS package from British Intelligence Software Company Limited.)

The Information Technology Opportunities

It was found out that the underlying information technology employed by Mono-Bank during the mid-1970s was the use of IBM's real-time operating system together with the Assembler Language-based on-line Savings and Current Accounts System. In order to make the system work faster, Mono-Bank had modified IBM's 370 operating system kernels. Up to mid-1980s, Mono-Bank was still using IBM equipment to support the majority of their information systems applications.

Back in Poly-Bank, GIS received a newsletter from IBM in December 1995 announcing that IBM's Systems Application Architecture would soon support interconnection of all IBM's processors operating in a network of nodes, with the capability for each individual node's application program to send and receive data from the other nodes. In addition, IBM also announced that the LU6.2 communications protocol would soon support commands sent from one node of the network to other nodes for Distributed Transaction Processing.

There was a general belief at Poly-Bank senior management that as at the beginning of 1995, not only were hardware costs greatly decreased, the amount of software for application development had also increased tremendously. Examples that they heard include:

1. third-party productivity development software for program development such as:
    a. Computer Associate's COBOL Optimizing Compiler,
    b. Applied Data Research's Easy-Retrieve Report Generation Language.
2. capability of hardware such as IBM's AS 400 that includes a complete set of relational database management system software and operation system support for terminal-based and secured operating environments.

Poly-Bank's senior management also believed in the third wave of database software technology, program development languages and information system application development tools such as:

1. Relational Database Management Languages,
2. Productivity-oriented 4th Generation Languages,

3. Menu-Based Application Generators etc. which should enable production of the bank's planned information systems products and services in such a way as a manufacturing plant's automatic production line.

The Socio-Technical Aspects of Information Systems and Technology

Results of the Poly-Bank Global Branches System Development during the Period January 1995 to March 1996

A Project Manager from GIS was sent over to selected overseas branches of Poly-Bank in January and February 1995 to find out the general branches requirements for developing a common application-based Global Branches System.

Despite some concerns made by the Senior Banking Officers in Malaysia, Middle East and India offices, GIS believed that the system should be applicable to all branches with minor modifications for individual offices.

In March 1996, after 600 man-months of programming effort (amounting to US$1.8 million) had been spent on the development of the AS 400-based PAGLOB system, the Senior Banking Officers in Malaysia, Middle East and India refused to accept it for replacement of their own version of ICL ME/29 and IBM System/34-based Poly-Bank Automatic Branch Information Systems.

Furthermore, other branches demanded over 30% of changes to the newly developed software due to the slow response as demonstrated by the test run in Poly-Bank's Tokyo Head Office in February 1996.

A Joint User-Data Processing Development Effort by Users and Information Systems Professionals

After further meetings between the Senior Manager of GIS and Poly-Bank's International Banking Officers in April 1996, a common agreement was reached:

1. The user aspects and the local requirements of all the branch

operations would be taken into consideration before a full-scale system is to be implemented.

2. Executive type of information database would be developed in addition to the current facilities to enable overseas branch executives to work on selected data from their branch database for consolidated reporting to the Head Office in Hong Kong.
3. End-user computing would be permitted once local executive requirements could be fulfilled by the development of local-office PC-based application.

A Participant-driven Progression

As Chief Information Officer of Poly-Bank Corporation

It is now Monday, 1 July 1996. You had accepted the position of Chief Information Officer (CIO) & Assistant General Manager of GIS in Poly-Bank Corporation as you believed in the viability of a Senior Business Executive becoming the CIO of the same business.

Your immediate terms of reference from the Group Staff Controller and General Manager of Poly-Bank were:

1. To oversee the actual operations of Poly-Bank's Information Services Group.
2. To link information technology with the bank's business strategy.
3. To execute the information technology interface for the bank's sophisticated information systems products and services.

The Information Systems Development Priority List

An immediate need for Poly-Bank's GIS is to relieve the large number of savings accounts customers who were seen queuing for cash transactions both inside Poly-Bank's 500 branches and outside Poly-Bank's PATELL terminals.

Over the next few years up to the year 2000, the priority development list for Poly-Bank's banking information systems products and services, as contained within GIS's internal memoranda, are as follows:

1. Improve the speed of the Retail Banking System, probably by rewriting the major database portion of the on-line savings modules.
2. Develop the Corporate Banking System for corporate customers to link up their company's personal computer terminals to Poly-Bank for direct debit and credit transactions on their accounts.
3. Modify and implement the Global Branches System in order for Poly-Bank to expand its international trade finance through their global branches.
4. Develop an Executive Information Systems Environment for Senior Banking Officers to make use of information technology products (both hardware and software) for their own manipulation, analysis and presentation of data.
5. Develop Decision Support System prototypes to allow Senior Banking Officers to engage in investment (financial) planning activities.
6. Develop an Expert System to allow Junior Banking Officers to operate on complex banking procedures such as credit-card limit approval and authorization based on knowledge from the Senior Banking Officers.

Future Directions

Your future directions and strategies in information systems planning, development, implementation, and information technology usage will determine the success or failure of Poly-Bank's intention to use information system/information technology as the corporation's competitive strategy.

Your first week of priority tasks should be:

1. To resolve the staff recruitment problems due to shortages of skilled information systems professionals and the problems of emigration.
2. To sort out the problems with the Global Branches System.
3. To set priorities for GIS's information systems development projects.

4. To update yourself on hardware/software and telecommunications concepts in order to bring in the best choices for Poly-Bank.

Over the next few days, you will meet and discuss with the bank's Senior Banking Officers and GIS's project management to discuss a number of business and information systems-related topics.

Questions for Discussion

1. What were the pros and cons of appointing a senior business executive as Chief Information Officer of an organization in this case study?
2. With reference to Poly-Bank's Group Information Services Organizational Chart (Figure 2), are there any weaknesses in the structure?

3. What should be the level of user participation to be incorporated into Poly-Bank's Group Information Services? Should full-time user-coordinators be used and what are the disadvantages, if any?

4. On the hardware/software side, should Poly-Bank choose only one computer vendor or should Poly-Bank choose multiple vendors? Why?

5. What should be Poly-Bank's corporate policy in terms of software development tools for corporation-wide development work?

6. What are the pros and cons for Poly-Bank to contract out systems development work to outside software house? Should Poly-bank employ contract staff to work within Group Information Services, or recruit more programmers at higher salaries?

7. For Poly-Bank's banking products, should proprietary software purchased or should in-house development be carried out?

8. Are IBM computers the only hardware and software solution for banking information systems? Conduct a survey on local banks to find out the hardware and software facilities based on publications.

9. In order for you, the Chief Information Officer of Poly-bank, to execute the information technology interface with the corporation's information systems products and services, it is important to write a memorandum to Poly-Bank's Group Staff Controller explaining the differences and the priorities for the following:
   a. Distributed Transaction Processing System
   b. Transactions-oriented Operational System
   c. Decision Support-oriented Information System
   d. Management Support-oriented Financial Management/Investment Planning System

10. What are the values of the end-users systems analysts and systems developers in a banking environment?

11. Is there any value in selecting users at Senior Banking Officers level to participate as full-time user-coordinators in the systems analysis and design process for Poly-Bank? (Think of these from a cost/benefits point of view)

12. As Chief Executive Officer of Poly-Bank's GIS, perform a SWOT (Strengths, Weaknesses, Opportunities, and Threat) analysis for GIS.

5

Computerization in Central Power Corporation

A. M. Whiteley

The company, Central Power Corporation, is in the utilities business, supplying electricity, appliances, contract wiring and after-sales services.

In 1996, there was a \$2 billion turnover on electricity consumption. Appliances and contract wiring accounted for \$190 million. There was no accurate database on revenue from servicing as it was subsumed under the billing section.

There are around 500 staff employed in the company. Of the office staff, 23 are Unit Clerks. The Unit Clerks are usually female, under 30 years of age, and many of them are married. The job of Unit Clerk makes one responsible for a wide variety of tasks concerning a designated unit or section. A Unit Clerk is expected to handle bills competently, work out *pro rata* charges, deal with telephone complaints (an ever-increasing part of the job), answer written and personal enquiries and deal with the daily correspondence which comes from outside the firm and from other departments, particularly Debt Collection.

Unit Clerks are recruited as generalists rather than specific types of clerk such as Records Clerk, Filing Clerk, Billing Clerk, etc. There is no expectation of being tied to one particular job and no developed sense of job demarcation. Thus, Unit Clerks can flexibly adapt to the changing requirements of the organization.

Central Power Corporation is unionized. The chief role of the union to date has been on the welfare and recreational side although there have been some positive outcomes recently when representation was made for more worker involvement in company decisions. There is a representative for the clerical staff in the union. A small Industrial Relations Committee deals with matters of negotiation, i.e. pay, hours of work and conditions. Issues which concern both the direct labour workers and staff such as safety at work, training, and productivity are dealt with by a number of advisory committees. Employee representatives are elected. Management representatives are nominated. In addition to these arrangements, there are "understanding" meetings held around every three months and employees attend on a rota basis. The employee who attends tells his/her co-workers the meeting's content. One way or another, there is the opportunity for every worker or staff member's voice to be heard. Because "understanding" meetings are cross-sectional, clerical staff can see and hear about activities organization-wide.

Pay policies have presented no problem up to now. The non-supervising Unit Clerk can be paid at three levels, graded by job responsibility. Top-level pay is usually achieved within two years. Clerical work measurement and judgements on the responsibility level of the job serve as the pay base. This method enables a balanced weight of work to be measured and spread evenly among the clerks. A bonus is paid to staff in those sections agreeing to clerical work measurement. Assistant was provided by outside consultants when the system of clerical work measurement was introduced. The staff are at liberty to comment on or enquire about any aspect of the work measurement system.

Work methods in utilities companies are very similar in nature. Central Power Corporation faces competition from "Gas" and, indeed, from other clerical-intensive organizations. Central Power faces the all-too-familiar problems of recruitment, retention and replacement. The strong local economy means that Central Power is facing increasing competition in the labour market from banking, shipping, and insurance organizations. In response, it has attempted to make the Unit Clerk's job as attractive, interesting and varied as possible, as well as to provide good office equipment.

Still, the volume of work increases. Several thousand bills are sent to customers every month and the number is growing rapidly.

Figure 1: Organizational Structure of Central Power Corporation (Staff)

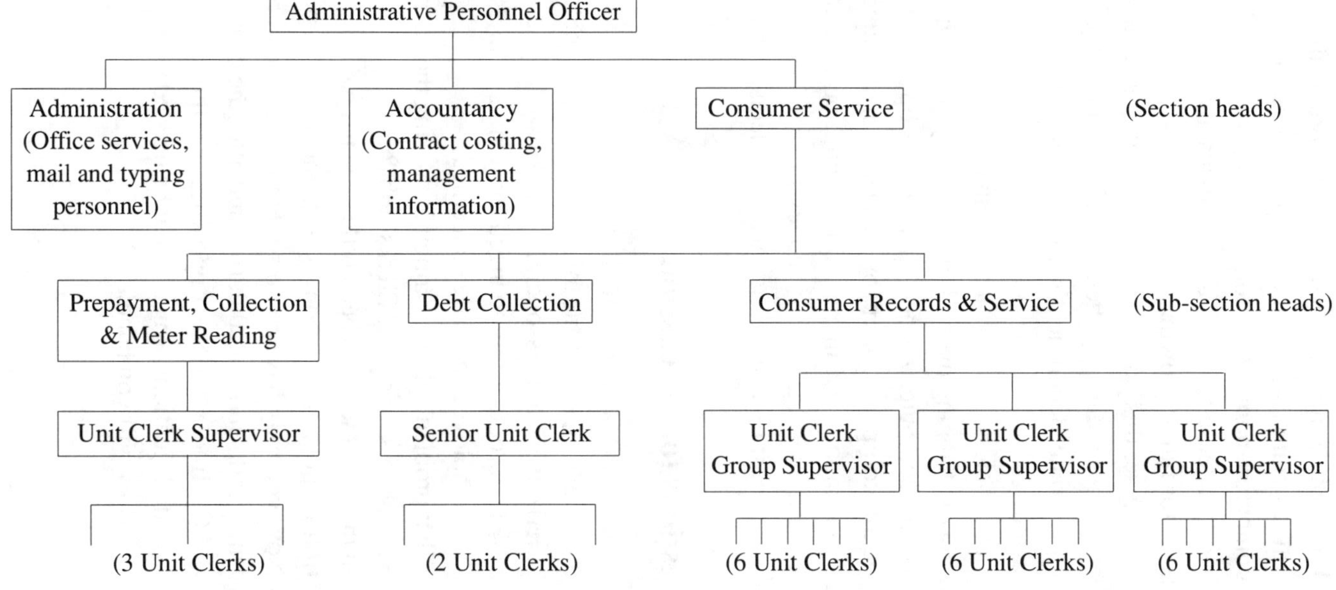

For some time now, it has been evident that while the existing clerical structure can just about cope with the present volume of work, the computerization of customer billing would be beneficial. It would lead to greater efficiency and, perhaps more importantly, a greater capacity for future growth.

Of course, this could not apply to interpersonal tasks such as consumer queries which, by their specific nature, have to be dealt with by the appropriate department's clerks. This problem would need to be addressed.

Nevertheless, senior management have decided to go ahead with the solution of changing the present clerical system in the consumer service section by computerization. There is the option either to recommend a type of computerization or to accept mainframe. Because of the healthy economy and increased consumption of electricity, appliances and contract wiring, there is money to spend on new equipment. This seems the most logical step to take. The decision has been made.

Questions for Discussion

1. You are the manager in charge of human resources development. You have a lend time of about one year before the first computerized system is operational. How do you develop strategies which introduce the changed system as painlessly as possible to those employees directly concerned?

2. What problems do you anticipate during the change-over regarding Supervisors' and Unit Clerks' jobs?

3. In the past, there has been little need to consider lack of job satisfaction or poor motivation as a threat to the company's well-being. Now you may have to do so. How might you continue to keep the Unit Clerks motivated during and after the change of system?

4. a. Outline possible opposition to the wage-payment system modifications which might be needed.

   b. How will you handle it?

6

Electronic Distribution of Hospital Supplies in Hong Kong

Robert Davison

In Hong Kong, there are a number of private and government hospitals. While they all provide medical services to the public, the way they charge for these services varies. On the other hand, in delivering their service to patients, all the hospitals need supplies of medical goods such as sheets, beds, surgical equipment, stationery and so on. In acquiring these essential items, the hospitals have a free hand, i.e. they can buy the items wherever they like so long as they meet strict government standards for quality.

At the present time, suppliers of these goods visit the hospitals on a more or less regular basis and take orders of supplies. The orders are processed by the supplier and a delivery is made, normally within seven to ten working days. The hospitals have complained that this is too long and that very often they need to get the goods faster; sometimes they have run their stocks dangerously low. The hospital suppliers, on the other hand, argue that seven days is really the fastest that they can do because it takes time to process the orders, gather the goods together and then send the goods to the hospitals. Occasionally, the goods need to come from overseas (e.g. for complex surgical equipment) and special arrangements have to be made both with overseas suppliers and air cargo operators, for such equipment must be handled very carefully and in a highly sterile environment.

A new company called Hong Kong Electronic Hospital Supplies (HKEHS) has recently been formed. It believes that it can take advantage of the present problems by radically changing the ordering and distribution market for hospital supplies in Hong Kong with the aid of Electronic Data Interchange (EDI).

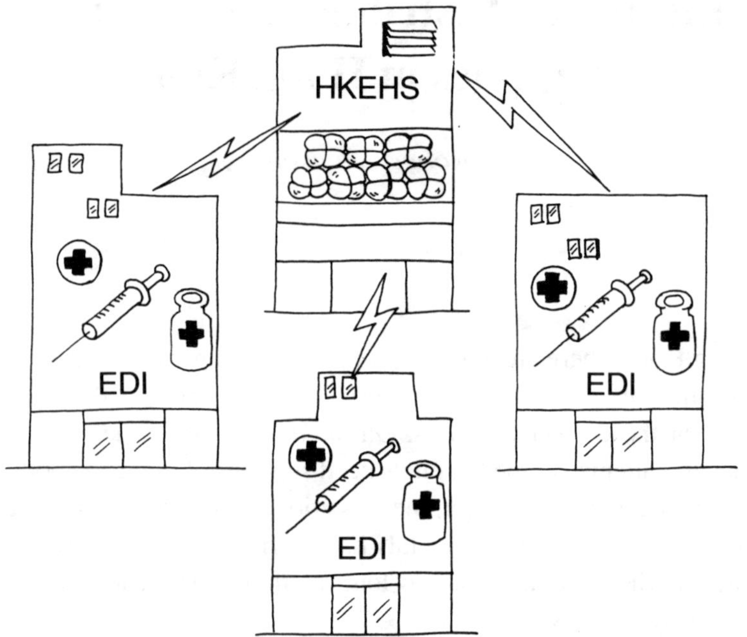

Question for Discussion

Using Porter's (1980) model of competitive forces as a framework, analyse how HKEHS can make use of EDI to penetrate the hospital supplies market and make the radical changes it believes are possible.

Your answer should include an explanation of the competitive forces model and an identification of the relevant forces in this case. You should also analyse which of these force(s) EDI is most likely to be able to exert an impact on so as to benefit HKEHS. Not all of the forces may be relevant to the solution. Be careful to identify which people or companies correspond to the different parts of Porter's model.

Try to identify potential problems with your solution for HKEHS, i.e. Where may there be difficulties? What might go wrong? What assumptions need to be made? What agreements will HKEHS need to make?

Part III

Ethical Issues

7

Software Piracy

Robert Davison

Golden Storehouse is an enterprise in the booming South Chinese city of Dongguan. The Chief Executive Officer and owner is Wong Kaiming, a local entrepreneur with influential connections in markets around the world. Recently CDs (compact discs) have been in high demand in Hong Kong where they are used both in the musical industry and the computer software/multimedia business. Two months ago, Mr. Wong decided to make a strategic business investment, quadrupling the production capacity of his CD plant. He has also made contact with local distributors in Hong Kong, requesting that they prepare for a flooding of the CD market. This means that they have taken on many temporary staff who will sell the CDs from trolleys on the streets of Mong Kok and elsewhere.

Chief Inspector Cheung of the Hong Kong Government's Customs and Excise Department has the responsibility of monitoring traffic flows through the China–Hong Kong border-crossing points. There has been an upsurge in smuggling recently, particularly of high-volume, mid-cost consumables such as CDs. Over 200,000 CDs can be packed into a single 40-feet container. Thousands of such containers pass through the border each day and only a fraction can be inspected.

Legitimately produced musical CDs, such as those manufactured by Phillips and Chandos, cost around HK$110 in Hong Kong. Pirated versions have street-market prices only one-third or a quarter the prices of their original real products, yet a container load is still worth around HK$6 million. The difference is even greater for computer software

CDs. CDs illegally imported from China are often shipped directly out of Hong Kong's container port, the busiest in the world, to overseas markets.

While Mr. Wong has decided to increase the number of pirated CDs reaching Hong Kong's ever-thirsty local and re-export markets, China has decided to crack down on the pirates. New laws have been enacted such that copyright violators can be sentenced to lengthy jail terms. The United States, which is concerned about the illegal CD trade and its loss of revenue, approves of this action. The Chinese authorities hope that this will stem the flow of CDs and also improve trade relations with North America. At the same time, they are negotiating a deal which will see the cost of legitimately produced CDs drop, thereby enabling a larger sector of the consumer market to be able to afford to buy CDs. With cheaper CDs on the market, as well as a strong legal deterrent, the incentive to pirate will quickly disappear.

Questions for Discussion

1. List the relevant facts in the above case.
2. List the relevant stakeholders in the above case.
3. Isolate the ethical issues in the above case.
4. Isolate the legal issues in the above case.
5. Do you think that the new initiatives being enacted by the U.S. and Chinese Governments will be effective? Please explain the implications of these initiatives for the various stakeholders.

8

Data Privacy in a Hospital

Robert Davison

Sui Yuen Hospital (SYH) is a large urban institution known for its efficient management of resources. The Information Systems Department's mainframe computers at SYH contain all patient data records. These can be accessed anywhere in the hospital through terminals in rooms that are locked when not in use. Only registered nurses and doctors have keys to access these rooms.

One of the busiest areas in SYH is the Accident and Emergency Department. This is the place where all the traffic accident victims are brought to, where life and death are separated by a thin line.

On her computer screen, Registered Nurse Sarah Yip is reviewing the case of Wong Fat-shing, a container-truck driver whose vehicle jackknifed at high speed on Lung Cheung Road. Since he was not wearing a seat-belt, he was thrown through the windscreen and rolled down a steep concrete slope at the side of the road. He suffered multiple injuries and is listed as being in critical condition.

After reading the information about his condition and the drugs he is being prescribed, Nurse Yip taps the space-bar so as to go to the next page. Tapping the space-bar also tells the computer that she is still working at the terminal. The system has been designed so that a screen automatically goes blank if a user does not interact within 60 seconds.

Suddenly the personal alarm system sounds an alarm — "Red Alert! Red Alert! Room 55! Sarah reacts immediately." She leaves the terminal and, without locking the room, runs off to the emergency in

Room 55. "Red Alert" emergencies take priority over all other events and so not locking the door is standard procedure.

Rosie Chang is a Student Nurse in the hospital. She hopes that one day she too will be a Registered Nurse. She has been helping in the hospital for one month now, bringing ice water, making beds, and comforting patients. She heard the "Red Alert" call, so she knows where all the nurses have gone. She sees the terminal switched on and goes to read the screen.

"Ah! Mr. Wong. Such a nice man. His eyes are so expressive. Lets see what it says about him. Multiple injuries. Blood type O. HIV positive. What? HIV positive? He's got AIDS? ..." The screen goes blank and Rosie walks out of the room just as Sarah Yip comes back.

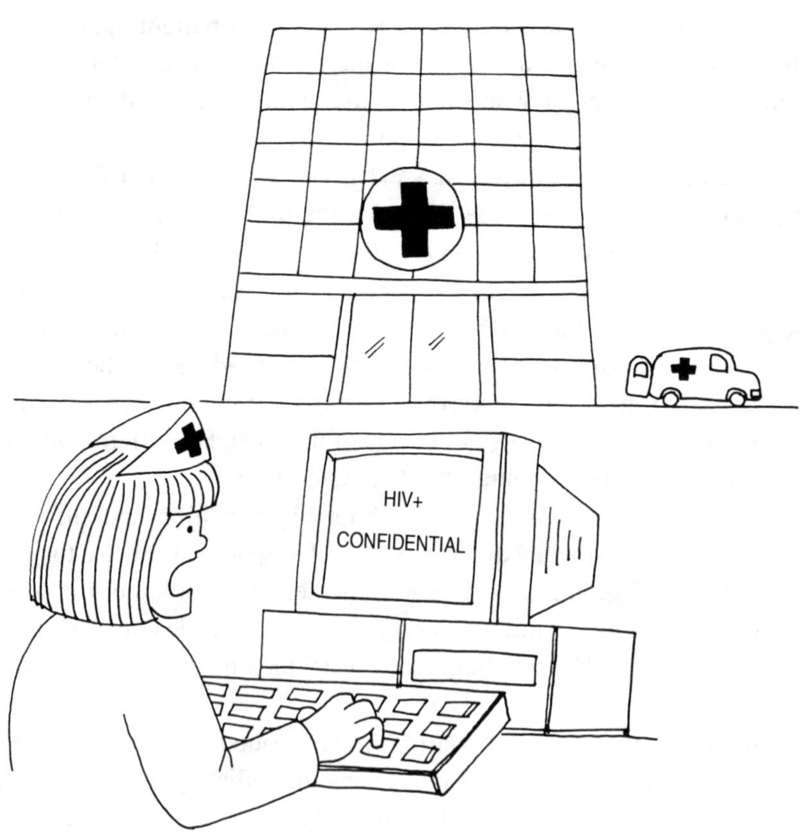

"Ah, Rosie. There you are. Mr. Wong asked specifically to see you when you arrived. He is so grateful for all the help you have given him…. What's the matter? …"

"Well, I'm sorry. Maybe I have spent too much time with him and ignored the other patients. And, besides, I might get AIDS."

"Rosie, what do you mean? Why do you think that?"

Questions for Discussion

1. What are the causes for the record of Mr. Wong to be observed by Rosie Chang?
2. List the relevant stakeholders in the above case.
3. Isolate the ethical issues in the above case.
4. Isolate the legal issues in the above case.
5. What steps should be taken to resolve the current situation? What kind of policies are needed to make sure that this problem does not occur again? Please explain the implications of the steps/policies.

Part IV

System Operation

9

The Computer System in PEC

E. Jordan

Introduction

PEC is a successful company, having grown to be one of the largest specialist electrical contracting companies in Hong Kong. Its business consists of installing electrical systems in industrial settings such as shipyards, container bases, large factories and materials-handling environments. It employs a number of electrical engineers, electricians and labourers who spend most of their time on site together with administrative staff, sales representatives and managers who usually work at Head Office. The General Manager is considering a computer system because a number of areas in the business are causing some concern, e.g. reducing profitability, and restrictions for expansion.

Tenders

The company's jobs are usually won by submitting a tender specifying the costs, although some jobs are obtained without submission of a tender. The costs are for labour and materials used on the job. Material items that are needed specifically for a job (that is, items not kept in stock) will be itemized in the tender. Stock items will be shown as single items in the tender. For the purpose of estimation, labour will be broken down into categories depending on the skills needed by the worker. Some tenders show each of these categories but others show just a single item for labour. Extensions to previous jobs may be awarded without competition and every contract has provisions for a "rise-or-fall" or "variation" to be negotiated at any time.

A "rise-or-fall" is an agreed increase or decrease in either one or both of the materials costs and labour costs as a result of circumstances outside the control of either party, such as a general pay rise granted to all electrical workers or a decrease in the world price of copper. Hong Kong or internationally published indexes are used as the reference point for these rises or falls and they are mentioned explicitly in the contract. The idea of a general, externally initiated pay increase may not be strictly applicable to Hong Kong but this facility in the "rise-and-fall" provision will add flexibility to the system.

A "variation" is (usually) an additional amount that may be charged when some impediment or complicating factor is discovered as job is progressing. An example of this is the discovery of rock that needs to be removed by pneumatic drill, found during excavations for the foundations of an electrical transformer. A variation may also be an extension of the original work decided while the job is in progress.

The quotation for the original tender and for any subsequent variations is prepared by an electrical engineer using the tender specification and a schedule of standard costs of labour and materials which is maintained by the engineers. Often estimates are used or the engineer may telephone a supplier to get a verbal quotation for a specific item that is required. A copy of the tender, as submitted to the prospective customer, is retained on file together with any supplementary information used by the engineer in preparing the tender.

Job Master File

If the tender is successful, a job master file is created. On the cover of this file, fixed information relating to the contract is noted while copies of all purchase orders, invoices, requisitions, time sheets and progress claims are stored inside the file. The inside cover is used to accumulate costs incurred in the job. If space runs out, additional sheets are stapled to the inside cover. The job master file in its physical form resembles manilla folders. There are preprinted spaces on the outside and inside covers for the entry of accumulated data. When the inside cover space is full, a new sheet with the same preprinted headings is stapled to the cover so that the original information is not lost and accumulation may continue.

Purchase Orders

These are orders to suppliers for specific materials that will be used on a particular job or for the replenishment of stock. The item may be as simple as an electrical switch or as large and expensive as a high-voltage transformer. It is company policy that nothing is to be requested or purchased from any supplier without a valid order number. The purchase orders are recorded in a three-part order book which has preprinted sequential numbering. This book shows the order number, date issued, job number, supplier name, item description and quantity. There is also a space to enter a quoted or agreed price but this is not always used. Every person authorized to order supplies is allocated an order book. Every week these books are shown to the administration clerks who remove the second copy so that the job master file may be amended.

A register of all purchase orders is kept by the administration office showing to which job each purchase order belongs. This register is in purchase order number sequence and includes the supplier name and date of issue. Sometimes a purchase order may contain a number of items but this rarely exceeds five; in fact the majority of orders contain only a single item.

Purchase orders for major items are issued by the engineer as soon as the tender is accepted but the majority of purchase orders are issued by the foreman, often over the counter at the supplier's premises. There is no formal division of responsibility between the foreman and the engineer for raising purchase orders. When the engineer creates a tender proposal, he will include (generally for internal use only) a complete list of all items and labour that will be needed. The material items will include both stock items and those for which a special purchase will be necessary.

When he is advised that the tender has been successful, the engineer will pass the tender to the Administration Department to check the list of materials. He raises purchase orders for items that he thinks should be ordered, based on the expected time for delivery.

When the foreman is allocated the job, he will also be given a copy of the tender, the specifications and the list of materials. He will then have the chance to raise purchase orders if necessary. He will get some items from stock and other items by driving to the supplier's premises and ordering and receiving the goods on the spot. If the job is not completed on schedule, then the manager will tend to blame both the engineer and the foreman.

Supplier Invoices

Suppliers will normally send one invoice for each purchase order but are not required to do this. Generally, multiple deliveries from the same purchase order will lead to a number of invoices. In addition, one invoice may refer to a number of different purchase orders depending upon the supplier's clerical system. A photocopy of each invoice is placed in the appropriate job file and the value of the goods is entered inside the job file cover. The job number is determined from the purchase order number which is usually quoted on the invoice.

The original invoice is stamped with a rubber stamp that leaves spaces to be filled in for verifying that the goods were received, the purchase order number, the date invoice received and the date passed for payment. When this process is completed, it will be filed in supplier name sequence ready for the monthly payment routine. If the invoice offers a prompt payment discount, then it is filed separately into the "urgent" file that must get special approval from the Accountant. Any urgent items are processed individually with a cheque and remittance advice being typed by an accounts clerk.

The decision to put outstanding creditor invoices into the "urgent" file is made by the Accountant. She will base this decision on the importance of keeping good relations with the supplier and other factors such as the supplier's ability to force a payment (for example, an electricity or telephone company).

The monthly payment routine for all other invoices is done in a number of stages. Firstly, the values of all outstanding invoices are totalled to determine the total amount payable. If this is within the limit of the available funds determined by the Accountant, then remittance advices and cheques will be prepared for all outstanding invoices. If the amount required exceeds the available funds, then subtotals of amounts payable are prepared for the major suppliers. Usually a few big invoices will be deferred to bring the total amount down to an acceptable figure. Then the remittance advices and cheques are prepared as above. All deferred invoices will be marked so that they are not deferred again next month, and a number of them will be placed in the urgent file so that they can be paid as soon as possible. A remittance advice is sometimes known as a remittance slip. It is a document that accompanies a payment informing the recipient of the payee, the amount and the reason for the payment.

Monthly statements sent by the suppliers are filed in supplier name sequence together with all invoices that have been paid and the copy of the remittance advice. These statements are only referred to in the case of disputed payments as PEC pays by invoice rather than by statement.

Requisitions

These are paper dockets of vouchers that are used to take supplies from the inventory of standard items. Many jobs require screws, fasteners, wire, piping, ducting and other sundry items. This is held in stock in sufficient quantities to meet most normal demand. Any job requiring abnormally large quantities of such items will necessitate raising a purchase order specifically for that job.

The store clerks raise purchase orders for replenishment of this stock based on a visual stock check. Each shelf, bin, or container is marked with a red line which indicates that the critical stock level has been reached. An order is raised each day for all items that have reached the critical level. When the goods on a requisition have been supplied, the store clerks will price each item supplied by referring to their master price list which is kept up to date by the store clerks who acknowledge the receipt of goods when the invoice is received from the supplier.

Time Sheets

When work actually commences on a job, it is the responsibility of the Site Foreman to keep and submit time sheets for all workers. The employee will not be paid in full without time sheets covering the full working day. A time sheet is kept for each job number. Each line on the time sheet refers to an individual employee. The employee name and number are entered together with the start time, stop time and number of ordinary hours and overtime hours for each working day. The time sheets are signed by the Foreman at the end of the week and sent to the office. In some cases, the customer's Site Supervisor will also sign these sheets. Any bonuses or allowances to which an employee may be entitled are calculated and entered in extra columns by the staff in the Administration Office.

The sheets are then photocopied with the original being sent off to a computer bureau for production of payslips, pay advices, payroll reports, job cost report and cash analysis. These are returned to the office by Thursday so that pay envelopes with the correct amount of cash can be prepared for collection of Friday by the Foreman and distributed to the employees on the same day. The employees are not paid in their first week of employment but are paid for the previous week actually worked.

The job cost report shows each employee's hours that have been charged to the job with the amount paid, with a subtotal for each job. This is received from the computer bureau in two copies: the first is filed in date order; the second is cut into sections for each job number. These sections are filed in the job master file and the amounts are entered, along with the week-ending date, on the inside cover of the file.

Progress Claims

As a job moves towards completion, certain stages are reached where the contract allows for partial payment of the contract value. This invoice to the customer is called a progress claim. In most cases, they are for fixed amounts that were stipulated in the contract; however, in certain cases (small jobs, variations, etc.) the progress claim will be for an amount calculated on the work done and materials used. These are usually known as "do-and-charge" jobs.

The labour rates charged are fixed in advance and a handling charge percentage is added for all materials used. This is applicable to the domestic and industrial electrical tool repair shop that the company operates adjacent to its main factory. "Final" progress claims are prepared when the job is completed. It is often necessary to wait for all supplier invoices specifying the costs of the items that were on the purchase orders to arrive. This delays the final progress claim for do-and-charge jobs and delays determining the job's profit or loss.

The progress claims are posted to the customer as soon as they are prepared, with a copy being filed in the "claim outstanding" file. Each month, statements are typed for each customer showing all out-standing progress claims. When a payment is received, the copies of the progress claims being paid are removed from the "claim outstanding" file, stamped "paid" and filed in the "claim paid" file, also in customer order.

Divisions

The company is organized into a number of divisions based on the type of work that is done. These are Maritime Division, Materials Handling Division, AGO Division, Repair Shop, AirCon Division and General Division. AGO Ltd. is PEC's single largest customer. The division established to give that customer a high standard of service is the AGO Division (not AGO Ltd.). The General Division looks after work that does not clearly fall into the area of responsibility of any of the other divisions. Typically, it may include work in the hotel industry, public housing construction industry, transport industry and certain Govern-ment departments. Note that the manager of the General Division is not the General Manager (GM) who runs the business. The Administration Department serves all clerical functions. The Accountant is the manager of this Department and she has the same status as a Divisional Manager. She allocates clerical tasks to the staff under her control.

The Stock Department is under the management of the Repair Shop Manager. A purchase order book is kept in that Department for reordering stock items. It has its own job numbers, which are in the "overhead" category.

With the exception of the Repair Shop, all departments employ electrical engineers and some employ sales representatives (two in AirCon, one in each of General, Maritime and Materials Handling). The Manager of each Division reports directly to the GM who in turn reports to the company owners. All contracts are signed by the GM. The GM is responsible for overall profitability which is achieved mostly by carefully controlling costs and by monitoring the value of work-in-progress.

Any cost incurred within the organization is charged to a job number. This may be an "overhead" job number for central administrative functions or a "non-productive" job number such as "waiting at workshop" or "absent — sick leave."

An overhead job number is a number that is used to allocate costs and expenses that are not part of a particular contract. Every item of cost and expenditure within the organization is charged to a job number. In many ways these are similar to the idea of cost codes or general ledger expense categories used in other businesses. The Administration Department uses the term "job number" for all expenses.

The GM expects to receive a report for each completed job showing each item of expense and revenue and an analysis of the job's profitability. These reports are usually prepared as a batch at the end of the month and are generally ready by the tenth working day of the month after the jobs are completed. When these have been scrutinized and accepted by the GM, they are then assembled into Divisional and company reports for the owners. It is not unusual for the GM to find charges that have not been passed on to the customers or other errors. Some of these can still be corrected but for some of them it is too late; the customer will not accept additional charges. This represents a continuing irritation to the GM and he wants to improve the method of control for charging so that nothing is missed. This is one reason that a computer is being considered.

As the workload in each Division varies depending upon the number of jobs currently being undertaken, it is quite normal for employees to be moved between Divisions. This only applies to the various grades of electricians and labourers, not to the sales representatives and engineers. Normally employees will only be moved from one Division to another when a job is completed. Foremen, engineers and sales representatives are rarely transferred between Divisions as they tend to develop expertise in their particular areas. Electricians and labourers may be transferred because of work pressure, as it is quite straightforward for the foremen to give them tasks within their expertise while they are settling in.

In order to allocate the costs of administration back to the Divisions, the total revenue of each Division is determined each year and the total administration cost is distributed evenly in proportion to the Division's revenues. Unfortunately, this masks the inefficiencies of certain Divisions by not attributing the actual costs of administration that they have generated. This represents a continuing point of argument between Divisional Managers.

In general, activity between Divisions is so small that it may be ignored.

Work in Progress

This is the value of work that has been commenced but has not yet been invoiced to the customer. In other words, it is the value of progress claims that could be made if all jobs currently under way were to be invoiced for the value of work that has been done to date. Typically, the Accountant will use a cut-off date — the last working day of the month — to ascertain which jobs are not complete, to calculate (or estimate) the labour and materials costs incurred and to add on the appropriate margin to determine the work-in-progress value. If some progress claims have been made, then only work done after the last progress claim is included. The value of work-in-progress is included as an asset in the Balance Sheet where financial reports are prepared.

Repair Shop

The Repair Shop originated as a small workshop within the main building where power tools used by the various Divisions were repaired.

Making this area accessible to the public opened up a new area of business. Very few tools belonging to other Divisions are now repaired here. The Repair Shop does not prepare tenders, does not employ a sales representative nor an engineer but operates in a simple fashion, repairing power tools and charging for the time and materials used ("do and charge"). Members of the public are expected to pay on the spot when collecting repairs; established customers will be sent invoices and monthly statements. Job master files are not used here; a simple job sheet is sufficient.

Location

The company is entirely located at a single building except for a small site office at the premises of AGO Ltd. This building has offices for all the managers, engineers, sales representatives and the Accountant together with the administration staff. The inventory store is also in this building together with a large workshop where any items that may be prefabricated are manufactured (such as power control switchboards etc.). This site office at AGO is provided mostly out of hospitality.

Computer bureau

The computer bureau is an outside commercial organization which provides a service (payroll processing) for money. It has other services available but has specialized in payroll. Its payroll programs are extremely reliable and provide an excellent service. Time sheets are submitted to them, they are then keyed in, validated and processed. Master files and transaction files are kept at the computer bureau. In addition to the time sheets, data sheets for master file maintenance (addition, changes, deletions of employees, rates of pay, etc.) and correction to previous weeks' payrolls are submitted. There are large variety of reports that are available but as the charges increase for each additional report, usually only payslips, pay envelopes, payroll analysis, cash analysis and job cost reports are requested.

Table 1: Statistics on the Operation of the Company

Productive work	Repair shop	Other divisions (average)
Average number of jobs in progress at any one time (in the division)	2.2	4.4
Average number of employees working on an individual job	1	4.2
Average number of purchase order/job	0.2	300
Average number of invoices/purchase order (multiple deliveries)	1.0	1.6
Average number of purchase orders per invoice (multiple purchase orders quoted)	1.5	1.1
Average job duration (man-hours)	0.8	1,140
Profit margin (PM) on labour cost	120%	100%
PM on materials cost	40%	20%
PM on requisitions cost (stock)	40%	15%
Labour as a percentage of total charge	70%	50%
Material as % of total charge	20%	40%
Stock requisitions as % of total charge	10%	10%
Active customers per year (total)	1,200	50
Number of suppliers (total)	100	600
Debtors average days outstanding	24	62
Creditors average days outstanding	40	40
Number of tenders submitted/month	0	0
Percentage successful tenders	n.a.	approx. 50%
Average variations per contract	n.a.	1.9
Average rise-and-fall claims/contract	n.a.	0.4
Percentage do-and-charge of total $	100%	18%
Average daily wage	$180	$210
Average overtime hours per week	8	6
Overheads — Divisional Manager daily wage	$395	$420
Engineer daily wage	n.a.	$340
No. of engineers per Division	0	2
Sales representative daily wage	n.a.	$90
No. of sales representative per Division	0	1–2 (AirCon), 0 (AGO)
Sales representative commission (on total charge)	n.a.	1.4%
Vehicle running costs per annum	$10,000	$115,000 per Division
Employee unproductive hours per annum (includes sick time, excludes holidays)	160	220
Workers' compensation insurance (percentage of total wages)	3%	4%

Table 2: Central and Administration Costs

General

Normal hours per week all employees	40
Length of working day	8 hours
Paid annual leave	10 days
Paid public holidays	12 days
Overtime pay factor (no overtime paid to managers, engineers or representatives)	1.5

Store

Average stock holding	$120,000
Increase over previous year	11%
Number of stock clerks	2
Average daily wage	$132
Average weekly overtime	3.4 hours
Number of stock items	1,150

Administration

GM daily wage	$700
Accountant daily wage	$390
Clerks (12) average daily wage	$148
Average overtime per week	2.2 hours
Phone, electricity, stationery, etc.	$40,000 per month
Rental, insurance, vehicle lease, etc.	$270,000 per month
Vehicle running costs	$70,000 per annum
Computer bureau costs	$90,000 per annum
Overdraft interest (rate say 7%)	$262,000 per annum

Questions for Discussion

1. What are the problems associated with the issue of purchase orders?
2. What are the problems associated with the handling of supplier invoices?
3. What other management problems can you identify with the current operational system of PEC?

10

City School's Student Admission System

P.K.O. Chow, Y. K. Chow and S. W. Li

Introduction

City School (CS) is a tertiary institution that occupies a newly built and fully equipped campus and provides higher education opportunities for secondary school-leavers in Hong Kong.

Being a major institution in higher education, CS admits around 3,000 students annually. However, owing to fierce competition for admission, up to 30,000 applications are normally received. It has long been a headache for the CS administration to process this large volume of applications. To further aggravate the problem, these applications have to be processed within a short time frame. This is usually after the announcement of public examination results in July and before the beginning of the academic year in October.

The following sections elaborate on the manual processing of the current admission system at CS.

Admission System Outline

The admission procedures are comprised of a series of steps in the processing of application forms, selection of applicants and offering of course admission.

Applicants request blank application forms from the Admission Office. The Admission Office record names and addresses of the applicants before sending them the application forms. Applicants return the completed forms to the Office who validate the applications by checking entry requirements and then prepare acknowledgment letters. They then send out letters inviting the qualified applicants to attend an interview. The application forms from applicants are also sent to the academic departments so that they can prepare for the interviews.

The academic departments conduct the interviews and compile a list of successful applicants. This list is then passed to the Admission Office.

The Office send offers to the successful applicants and inform the academic departments once they receive an applicant's response. Departments then prepare course lists.

Detailed Admission Procedures

In May of each year, CS starts to accept applications for the various study programmes that it offers. Any applicant can visit the Admission Office to get a free application form, which comes in duplicate copies. Table 1 is an example of this. Alternatively, the applicant can send a stamped, self-addressed envelope to the Admission Office. In all cases, they record the applicant's name and address in a log book.

After completing the two copies of the application form and attaching references, an applicant returns his or her application form to the Office. After receiving the completed application form, the Office validates the data on the forms. Once a form has been validated, the minimum entry requirements for admission are checked.

When all checking has been done, an acknowledgment letter is sent to inform the applicant that his or her application is being considered for further processing. An example is shown in Table 2. An application record will also be set up in the Admission Office. At present, it is the policy of CS that all qualified applications, numbering around 80% of total applicants, will be granted interviews. The Admission Office will update the First Interview Call field in the Admission Application file.

The departmental copies of the qualified candidates will be transferred to the department of first choice. When the departments receive these records, they will enter them onto the Departmental Application files. Departments then send an interview list to the Admission Office for preparing and sending out interview letters. An example can be seen

Table 1: Application Form of City School

<table>
<tr><td colspan="2">PERSONAL PARTICULARS</td><td>For Office use only
APPLICATION no.: 89 __</td></tr>
<tr><td colspan="3">
SURNAME: _______________________________
FIRST NAME: _______________________________
HONG KONG ID: _______________________________
DATE OF BIRTH: __________ / __________ / __________ (DD/MM/YY)
SEX: _______________________________
ADDRESS: _______________________________
____
TELEPHONE: _______________________________
</td></tr>
</table>

COURSES APPLIED FOR

	Course Code	Year Apply	Course Title
FIRST CHOICE	__________	__________	__________
SECOND CHOICE	__________	__________	__________
THIRD CHOICE	__________	__________	__________

QUALIFICATIONS

MATURE APPLICANT: (Y/N) __________
TECHNICAL INSTITUTE ATTENDANCE: (Y/N) __________
TECHNICAL INSTITUTE CODE: __________
COURSE CODE/YEAR: __________ / __________
PUBLIC EXAMINATION: (HKCEE = 1, HKHLE = 2, HKALE = 3)

	Subject	Grade	Exam. Code	Year
1.	__________	__________	__________	__________
2.	__________	__________	__________	__________
3.	__________	__________	__________	__________
4.	__________	__________	__________	__________
5.	__________	__________	__________	__________
6.	__________	__________	__________	__________
7.	__________	__________	__________	__________
8.	__________	__________	__________	__________
9.	__________	__________	__________	__________
10.	__________	__________	__________	__________
11.	__________	__________	__________	__________
12.	__________	__________	__________	__________
13.	__________	__________	__________	__________
14.	__________	__________	__________	__________
15.	__________	__________	__________	__________
16.	__________	__________	__________	__________
17.	__________	__________	__________	__________
18.	__________	__________	__________	__________
19.	__________	__________	__________	__________
20.	__________	__________	__________	__________

Table 1: (Cont'd)

For Office Use Only		Choice		
		1st	2nd	3rd
INTERVIEW CALL:	(Y/N)	_______	_______	_______
INTERVIEW RESULT:	(Y/N)	_______	_______	_______
APPLICATION DECISION:	(Y/N)	_______	_______	_______
APPLICANT RESPONDE:	(Y/N)	_______	_______	_______
GRADE POINT SCORE:	(Y/N)	_______		
STUDENT NUMBER:	(Y/N)	_______		
COURSE CODE/YEAR:	(Y/N)	_______ / _______		

DISTRIBUTION COPIES:

ORIGINAL (WHITE)   — ADMISSION OFFICE

DUPLICATE (BLUE)   — ACADEMIC DEPARTMENT

Table 2: Acknowledgement Letter of City School

Date:
Name:
Address:

Dear Applicant,

Please be informed that your application for admission to City School has been received and is being considered for further processing. We will keep you informed on the progress of your application in due course.

Thank you for the interest shown to City School.

Yours sincerely,

Admission Office
City School

in Table 3. The departments will then update the First Interview Call field in the Departmental Application files.

Applicants will come to CS for interviews at the times stated on the interview letters. Academic departments have to decide during the interview whether to recommend or reject the applicant. The Interview Result field will be updated accordingly. If the number of recommended applications is greater than the admission quota, the recommended applications will be prioritized by grade point scores.

Each department will send a list of successful applicants together with a waiting list to the Admission Office. In the mean time, the department will update the Application Decision field in the Departmental Application file. When the Admission Office receives the interview report, it updates the Admission Application file and then sends out admission offer letters to successful applicants.

Successful applicants have one week to consider the admission offers before sending them back to CS. The Admission Office will try to make a phone call to clarify the status if it does not receive the return

Table 3: Interview Letter of City School

Date:
Name:
Address:

Dear Applicant,

We would like to invite you for an admission interview with details as follows:

  Date:
  Time:
  Place:

Thank you in anticipation of your prompt arrival.

Yours sincerely,

Admission Office
City School

letter within the specified date. They will update the Applicant Response field in the Admission Application file when they receive the applicant's response. If the applicant declines the admission offer, the Office will immediately send an offer letter to the next applicant on the waiting list. This process will be repeated until the number of positive responses exhausts the admission quota. The Admission Office will then inform departments about their applicants' responses.

Departments then set up a file of Departmental Student records based on responses from applicants. Data from the Departmental Application file will be transferred to the Departmental Student file. Prior to the commencement of the study programme, a course list of admitted applications will be prepared and distributed to course organizers.

Validation of Application Forms

The following items are checked on the application forms:

- Name and address presented on form
- References attached
- Course code and title stated correctly

Application forms without name and address will not be processed. A reject letter will be sent to those applicants who either did not correctly state their course codes and titles or did not attach references. An example is shown in Table 4.

Checking of Entry Requirements

An applicant who is over 25 years old and who has no formal qualifications can apply for admission as a mature applicant. No minimum requirement needs to be checked in this case. Otherwise, the applicant must have English and Mathematics at grade "C" or better in the Hong Kong Certificate of Education Examination (HKCEE) as the minimum entry requirement.

To apply for a particular study programme, an applicant must meet one of two criteria. The first criterion is an appropriate Technical Institute Diploma. The other criterion is the computed grade points of

Table 4:   Reject Letter of City School

Date:
Name:
Address:

Dear Applicant,

We would like to inform you with regret that your application for admission to City School has failed due to the following reason(s):

    _____   Inadequate information on the application form
    _____   Minimum requirements not met
    _____   Unsuccessful interview

Thank you for your interest shown to City School.

Yours sincerely,

Admission Office
City School

public examination results. An applicant must have at least a computed grade point of 45 in order to meet the minimum entry requirements. Details of grade point computation can be referred to the "Computation of Grade Points" section of Table 5. Any applicants who do not meet the entry requirement will receive a reject letter.

Computation of Grade Point

Subjects passed in the HKCEE at the highest grade, up to maximum of five, are selected. Mathematics and English grades must be included. The grade of each subject is converted into its corresponding grade point based on the conversion rules specified in Table 5. The grade points of all selected subjects are added together.

Then a maximum of three subjects with highest grades from either the Hong Kong Higher Level Examination (HKHLE) or the Hong Kong

Table 5: Computation of Grade Points

Grade	A	B	C	D	E
Point	5	4	3	2	1

Examination	HKALE	HKHLE	HKCEE
Weight	3	2	1

Advanced Level Examination (HKALE) are selected. The grade of each subject is converted into its corresponding grade points, also based on the conversion rules specified in Table 5. The grade points of all selected subjects are added together.

Different weights are assigned to the three public examinations. Details of the weight assignments are specified in Table 5. These weights are multiplied by the computed grade points for each public examination.

An applicant's final grade point will be the sum of the weighted grade points of all relevant public examination results.

Questions for Discussion

Based on the information provided in the case, prepare Data Flow Diagram (DFD) for the following systems:

1. The overall Admission System.
2. The detailed admission procedures including the processing of application forms, validation of application, acknowledgments, etc.
3. The detailed interviewing procedures including the selection of interviewee, computation of grade point, prioritizing interviewee, etc.
4. The detailed checking procedures including reference, course titles, etc.

11

Developing a Garment Manufacturer from Run-of-the-Mill to Top-of-the-Line

Robert Davison

Hong Kong is famous for fashions. Almost anywhere you go you will find boutiques selling a wide range of styles, mostly at relatively affordable prices. Moreover, people like to buy clothes frequently. So it is not surprising that there is both a large number of garment retailers and a healthy state of competition in the market-place.

Impresario Holdings is one such garment manufacturing and retail firm specializing in fashion items at the young end of the market. It has a design operation in a commercial building in Tsuen Wan, management and accounting operations in an office suite in Cheung Sha Wan and a factory in Fo Shan, Guangdong. All operations, both in Hong Kong and China, are fully computerized. Designs are taken from Hong Kong to China as required and the clothes are manufactured there. Currently, 145 staff are employed in Hong Kong and another 200 in China. For a long time, it has been doing little more than break-even on its turnover, i.e. there have been no real profits made. While it has a fairly reliable teenage customer base at the low end of the market, its retail outlets tend to be located in older buildings or in public housing estates with lower rents while its competitors have premises in newer, more flashy locations.

Top management has decided that the firm needs to be turned round so that it becomes a leading contender in the fashion market-place with substantial profit margins. At the same time, it will need to both redefine who its customers should be and consider a major reorganization of its Hong Kong structure.

Question for Discussion

Using an information systems approach, as well as with reference to appropriate models and frameworks for competition and growth, explain how Impresario Holdings can be transformed from a rather ordinary retail outlet to one that is admired and envied by the competition.

You should focus on both of the following two areas:

1. Marketing and advertising information systems in Impresario Holdings.
2. Quality control and the elimination of waste in manufacturing processes in Impresario Holdings.

In each area, you should identify the key questions which need to be addressed. You should also point out which issues are important and how those issues can be tackled with information systems.

Part V

Information Systems Development

12

To Outsource or Not to Outsource — B & E Banking Corporation

Eva Y. W. Wong

Part I

B & E Banking Corporation is one of the note-issuing banks in Hong Kong. Information technology is used extensively to support its diversified portfolio of banking and financial services to its customers. One of its most successful and thus most demanded financial services is in the area of loans. With the recent slow-down in the economy coupled with the tighter regime issued by the Hong Kong Government on house purchases, the number of applications on home-purchasing loans or mortgages has decreased significantly. As a result, the bank has unwittingly accumulated a huge surplus in cash. Management, realizing that this is not good for business, has decided to channel its funds and effort into personal/taxation loans.

The trouble with small loans like personal/taxation loans is that although the amount of cash involved with each customer may not be as large as that of a mortgage loan, the work associated with authorizing the loan is just as complicated. Each loan application starts with a completed application form. An assessor will be assigned to each application and he/she will usually arrange to interview the applicant. A number of questions will be asked at the interview, and the details on the application form also have to be verified. After the assessor has checked all related information, he/she will either reject or approve a loan with a specific amount. This kind of complicated approval procedure is acceptable for large loans like mortgage applications, but for personal/taxation loans the procedures involved are far too complicated. As the number of personal/taxation loans increases, more assessors are needed. Furthermore, competition in this sector of banking service is getting fierce, customers may be turned off by the seemingly inefficient process and take their business to another bank.

The information systems (IS) executive of the bank is asked to study the situation and suggest feasible solutions to management. The IS executive suggested that a credit-granting expert system should be developed for use in the approval of personal/taxation loans. Three experienced assessors will be seconded to work with IS professionals on this project. B & E Banking Corporation has a well-developed IS department managing its numerous information systems. However, the IS department does not have any experience in developing expert systems. Thus, the IS executive further suggests that the project can be developed in-house or its development can be outsourced to a software house.

Part II

The IS department is keen to develop the expert system in-house so that it can acquire the necessary skills and experience. It also wants to adopt a proper information systems development methodology (ISDM) for this project.

The project has finally been approved by management. During an interview session with the assessors, they said that they always ask loan applicants a number of questions relating to their current financial status in order to help them with the final decisions of rejecting or approving the applications. The questions they always ask cover the following areas:

- Income level of the applicant
- Existing mortgage payment
- Existing car payment
- Existing hire purchase payment (for example, VCR or hi-fi purchases)
- Any other debts
- Number of years with present employer

Questions for Discussion

Part I

1. What is outsourcing?
2. What are the advantages and disadvantages of outsourcing?
3. Under what circumstances should outsourcing be used for building information systems?
4. In the above case study, would you recommend the bank to outsource the development of the expert system? Why?

Part II

1. Suggest an information systems development methodology suitable for use in the above case study. Justify your choice.
2. Prepare one rule for each question that the assessors ask in the following format, and state any assumptions that you have made clearly:

IF: <condition>
THEN: <action or result>
REASON: <the rationale>

13

Information Systems Development Methodology — The Case of Wah Ming Electronics Limited

Eva Y. W. Wong

Wah Ming Electronics Limited is an electronic components manufacturer. It started business in Hong Kong in the early 1980s with a small factory in the New Territories.

Information technology (IT) was used to help with various operations from the start. As the business expanded and the company matured over time, an information systems (IS) department was set up to formalize IT strategies within the organization. The IS executive was an engineer by training; he believed that software development should be treated as an engineering process, thus the IS department had a systematic and formal way for developing applications, and Structured Systems Analysis and Design Methodology (SSADM) was the chosen information systems development methodology (ISDM). This way of system development worked well when the company was small and most of the users had a technical or engineering background.

As the company expanded, people of other disciplines such as business management and accountancy joined the organization. These new users had their own requirements for computer use but they were not accustomed to such a rigid development methodology. They had difficulty in understanding the terminology used by the analysts/ programmers. The analysts/programmers, on the other hand, could not get concrete system requirements from these users because the users could not specify what they want in a formal and consistent style. As a result, communications between these users and the IS department broke down. The users complained that the IS department could not provide any service to them. The IS department complained that the users did not know what they wanted. The IS manager buckled under the pressure and left the company.

A new IS manager joined the company. Noticing what was happening, she advised the IS executive that there are other system development methodologies available. She suggested that they should choose one which better suited the organization. However, they needed to understand the metaphors adopted by the users first. The IS executive was puzzled and wanted to know more.

Questions for Discussion

1. What is an information systems development methodology?
2. Define the term "metaphor" and explain its relevance in information systems development.
3. List the critical success factors in introducing a formal information systems development methodology to an organization.
4. What kind of information systems development methodology would you suggest to the company in the case study? Why?

14

Global Risk Management

Miranda Fan

Worldwide Finance Inc. was a U.S.-based merchant banking group specializing in securities trading activities. The head office was located in New York, with branch offices in Hong Kong and Sydney, Australia. Major activities of Worldwide Finance Inc. were tracing of various securities including bonds, certificate of deposits, commercial papers and perpetual notes, etc. In terms of volume of transactions, in 1996, the New York head office had an average daily transaction of 250 deals per day, followed by Hong Kong of 45 and Sydney of 20. Depending on the types of instruments, these deals had to be settled within two to seven days. Worldwide Finance Inc. also provided medium to long-term financing to corporate borrowers. Although this activity had been de-emphasized lately, it still required the support of Loan Administration.

In 1996, Worldwide Finance Inc. underwent a major international project to install a common computer system. The main objective was to enable the corporation to better manage its securities trading activities in the three offices. This was termed "Global Risk Management." There were a number of factors that had called for the need of such a system:

Forecasted Rapid Growth in Business

With the global securization trend of the debts market, it was projected that the business volume of both offices in Hong Kong and Sydney would increase significantly for the years to come. The number of deals per day in the Hong Kong office was expected to increase to 150 in 1997 and that of the Sydney office would rise to 130. The projected compound annual growth rate would not be lower than 30% from 1997 onward. Currently these two offices were using manual systems in handling securities settlement. Management information, e.g. asset portion, was rather inadequate. These would have negative impact on the growth and performance once the business volume expanded. Computerization was seen as the only way to support the business.

Coordination of Securities Trading among the Three Offices

Risk management is a crucial element in running a successful operation in securities trading. The New York office had been the centre for providing research facilities in analysis of economic performance, interest rate movements, currency trends and so on. However, day-to-day strategies taken by the three offices might be different, and naturally there was only limited coordination among the three offices as to how each should react to sudden and unanticipated changes in the market. This was exemplified by the fact that the New York office operated in a time zone which was different from that of Hong Kong and Sydney. Hence, a situation might arise when the New York office bought a certain instrument which the Hong Kong office had just sold. A global computer system was thus called for to provide a common database for the use of the three offices to enable better communication and better risk management through uniform and coordinated strategies. With different time zone, New York, Hong Kong and Sydney could have access to one another's asset portfolios. It would also enable trading activities to be performed in a more versatile manner. For example, the New York office could trade on the books of the Hong Kong or Sydney office when the latter were closed and vice versa.

In the areas of settlement, the New York office had been using a system called TEXT on an IBM minicomputer RS/6000. It had experienced great interface difficulties as the general ledger was running on DATAPOINT machine. As mentioned, both the Hong Kong and Sydney offices used manual procedures for settlement and faced the problem of saturation. All three offices were trying desperately to improve their respective management information system, and a global system with a database would be a solution to all these.

Integrated Accounting System

Each office had its own independent accounting system. New York office was running the accounting system under the DATAPOINT; Hong Kong and Sydney were running their general ledgers on IBM RS/6000 supported by IBM PC and application software. All three offices had no linkage of the accounting system, although New York had introduced a uniform accounting format to be adopted throughout the three offices. This required a lot of time-consuming communication and raised a lot of problems in coordination and control. A lot of manual adjustments were necessary in each office. At the corporate level, group consolidation was another problematic area.

It was expected that the new system would provide automatic transmission of data to and from the corporate office, solve the consolidation problem and produce financial statements more efficiently. Above all, it should enhance the provision of management accounting information to aid management in decision making.

Loan Administration

The three offices provided lending to corporate borrowers, both onshore and offshore. At the moment, each of them used a loan administration system developed by the head office which ran on IBM RS/6000. The system was a very sophisticated one and was developed at the time the corporation had its major activity in the lending business. The system provided building diary, interest calculation, generalization of accounting entries and very good control of audit programs. It also handled various forms of lending, e.g. Letters of Credit, Letters of Guarantee in a most efficient manner. The nature of business did not require inter-office communication. However, with the change of business philosophy, it was intended that the new global system should provide only subsistent level of loan administration.

After prolonged consideration and lengthy discussions among top management of the three offices, it was concluded that the new computerized system should provide a common but sophisticated database with advanced communication features so that the three offices can exchange data for better market information, control and coordination. This total approach should also result in lower overall costs for project development and subsequent maintenance. Modular subsystems with interfaces to the main system would then be built around the database to suit the local requirements.

Basic Constraints

Hardware Resources Required

Worldwide Finance Inc. was a true believer of IBM. All hardware had to be IBM or IBM compatible to suit long-term corporate strategy on system development. Needless to say, application software must be able to run on IBM computers.

Software Package Versus Tailor-made Program

Typically the corporation faced a "make or buy" decision. It was estimated that at least 1,000 man-months which would cost US$12 million would be needed to develop a tailor-made program for this global risk management project. The alternative would be to use existing ready-made software which could run on IBM machines. However, there was only one reliable integrated software package in the market that was developed to support this business. The software's name was "FORTUNE" and the cost of licensing was US$4.5 million for the three sites. The problem with ready-made software was of course that it did not provide a perfect solution. As the cost difference was substantial, the management considered that this was the right route to choose. A detailed study, which should end up with a firm recommendation of cost, time frame and system specifications was then required.

Feasibility Study

A small team of two was assigned to carry out the feasibility study in the New York head office. David Jones, an experienced computer specialist who has worked for 15 years at Worldwide Finance, was one of the overall project managers once it was decided to go ahead. Peter Fox, the assistant operations manager, was the other one. Again the intention was that he would assist Jones in the project. In fact, they had been the main driving force behind the scene, and were extremely eager to have the project off the ground.

In the course of their study, assistance would be sought from the operations staff of the other two offices in respect to specific local requirements. The team reported to a steering committee in New York. The committee members included the General Manager, the Financial Controller, the Operations Manager and the Director in charge of securities trading and banking. The minutes of the meetings of the committee were also copied to the general managers in Hong Kong and Sydney.

Jones and Fox commenced a high-level study in April 1996. They spent one month in New York and visited Hong Kong and Sydney right afterwards. In each office they interviewed the senior executives to determine the user requirements and the extent to which FORTUNE could meet with them. After spending a total of three months, they produced their report to the steering committee. Their result indicated that globally 60% of the needs would be fulfilled by the standard software package; another 20% would have to be met by enhancements on the package by the software supplier and the remaining 20% of the needs would have to be met by users' adaptation because the costs of modification would be too big. It was estimated that the cost of enhancement would be US$1 million. Because of the time constraint, it was decided that low-level study would not be carried out.

As for hardware, IBM RS/6000 SMP was recommended because it could support a database architecture and the more advanced communication facilities. The FORTUNE software also ran on IBM RS/6000 SMP. The cost of hardware, together with the necessary peripherals for the communication facilities, would be US$1 million for each office.

In the course of their study, they also revealed several problems. The New York office had been using the IBM RS/6000 and DATAPOINT for the production run. It might take considerable time and risks to change over the two systems to the new IBM RS/6000 SMP and the FORTUNE software. Since there was no pressing need for a better system, operations people are not very enthusiastic about the whole concept. Both Hong Kong and Sydney were using IBM RS/6000 and PCs plus a lot of manual procedures. This would entail less conversion problems but human problems tended to intensify: top management believed that the system could replace a lot of people and thus reduce the head count, which had been used as a criterion for the measurement of managerial effectiveness. Junior staff felt unease as they were afraid that their jobs would be at stake. Worst of all, Jones and Fox knew that the new system was not going to replace many pairs of hands. They tried very hard to convey the message to these people but it did not seem to vary their implanted expectation by much.

Having found it difficult to choose between the two evils, they finally decided to let urgency dictate priorities. Hong Kong was therefore chosen as the pilot site because of its pressing problems in securities settlement.

Project Approval

Jones and Fox finally presented their firm proposal. At the steering committee level they did not meet much resistance, as the top management already realized that the existing set-up of the operation was not sophisticated enough and could not cope with the rapidly changing market environment. If no action was taken, new strategies might not work out and could lead to serious financial losses. Moreover, the share price of the cooperation had been rather depressed for the last several months. There was a potential threat of being taken over. Andrew Porter, the president, was particularly supportive to this idea, though he was aware that certain directors, who dominated the Capital Expenditure Committee, might oppose spending such a sum of money. He therefore brought the proposal, walked round each committee member and sought support individually. Fortunately, perhaps helped by the take-over threat, the proposal gained sufficient support and approval was finally granted at the committee's August meeting. The committee also gave a directive that the project should be completed as soon as possible, in any case not later than the fiscal year 1997–1998, i.e. March 1998. A contingency sum of US$200,000 was also approved.

Project Planning

Set-up of Project Team

Jones was then formally appointed project manager reporting to the project steering committee. Fox became the assistant project manager and helped coordinating all activities. Working under Jones were two separate groups: the user representatives from the three offices and two data processing representatives, Jack Evans from New York and Y. K. Chan for Hong Kong and Sydney. It was also decided that since the pilot installation would be in Hong Kong, Chan, who had over ten years of operations experience, would gain sufficient knowledge in the FORTUNE software during the installation and could be seconded to Sydney to take care of its subsequent installation.

At local company level, individual project committees were set up for coordination of various activities, including site preparation and procedural changes. The committees were presided by the respective local general managers. The data processing representative of the regional project committee would play the role as the project coordinator of the local company to carry out the following functions:

1. Negotiate and arrange with vendor for the support of hardware installation and system software training.
2. Organize training on application usage and implement procedural changes.
3. Reorganize staffing for the new environment.
4. Coordinate site preparation for the hardware, installation of system and parallel run.
5. Communicate with other regional project teams.

Phases of the Project

It was decided that the Hong Kong installation would go first. Installations for Sydney and New York would go at the same time. Success with the initial Hong Kong installation was therefore of paramount importance.

The project was broken down into five phases:

- Phase 1 — Detailed systems design
- Phase 2 — System enhancement
- Phase 3 — Installation for Hong Kong
- Phase 4 — Installation for Sydney
- Phase 5 — Installation for New York

Major milestones were identified as follows:

- Project organization established   Aug. 1996
- System design completed   Oct. 1996
- System enhancement completed   Jan. 1997
- Hardware delivered to Hong Kong   Mar. 1997
- Installation in Hong Kong go "live"   June 1997
- Hardware delivered to Sydney   Dec. 1997
- Installation in Sydney go "live"   Jan. 1998
- Hardware delivered to New York   Dec. 1997
- Installation in New York go "live"   Jan. 1998
- Terminals of three offices hooked up   Feb. 1998

Firm orders were then placed with the hardware and software suppliers.

System Design and Development

System Design

Based on the results of the high-level study, Jones and Fox worked out the preliminary enhancement specifications of the systems. Copies were sent out in September 1996 to the three offices for comments. Evans and Chan coordinated this process at the respective offices. It was found that local offices had asked for far more enhancements than the high-level study had recommended. However, owing to budget constraints, both in terms of cost and time, Jones and Fox decided that they could only afford to enhance what were recommended in the high-level study. If more modifications were needed, they had to be done by cash office individually after the project had completed. The final write-up of the enhancement was sent to local project committees for endorsement. Although each office had some complaints, nobody wanted to stick his neck out. Finally, in October 1996, all general managers signed back the specifications for acceptance. The copy was then sent to the project steering committee at New York for ceremonial approval.

System Enhancement

The system enhancement project (Phase 2) took place in New York. The modification work was contracted to FORTUNE in November 1996. It was agreed that it would take three months to complete the enhancement. The contract stated that the one-time contract cost of US$1 million would cover the stated enhancement. Further modifications would be charged at US$500 per man-day. Jones considered this a good deal as he did not anticipate any further changes to the package. "All users have encored the enhancement already, why should they ever change their mind?" he told Fox. Both Jones and Fox left pretty much of the enhancement work in the hands of the software supplier. They then went on for holidays in turn.

When Jones came back from holidays, he found that several requests for clarifications were sitting on his desk. Fox and Evans were unable to solve these problems because they were too technical. FORTUNE's work, in the interim period, was rather restrained. Jones quickly solved these problems but delay has already been caused.

System Implementation

Testing of Program

The system enhancement was eventually completed in February 1997, one month behind the original schedule. To make up the time delayed, Jones decided to crash the user training simultaneously as the testing was taking place. Both the user training and the testing were to be conducted in Hong Kong, the location of the Phase 3 work. To preserve costs, Jones decided that no representative from FORTUNE would be invited to go to Hong Kong to participate in the trial run. Instead, FORTUNE's Hong Kong representative office would send its staff to the site. Jones, Fox and Evans all flew to Hong Kong in early March 1997 to participate in the trial run. However, the trial run could not start until mid-March because the Chinese New Year holidays had effectively delayed the fitting out of the computer room to them. They took the chance to visit a few merchant banks which has installed FORTUNE. To their surprise all these users had their system maintenance done via their group offices in New York, London or Tokyo. The local FORTUNE office was no more than a sales office. Jones began to worry.

During the trial run, several system errors were spotted. As the local FORTUNE representative office did not have any technical staff, all problems had to be fed to FORTUNE in New York through telexes and telephone conversations. Because of timing differences, the project team had to stay late in most evening in order to have instant two-way communication. The FORTUNE people there seemed to have problem in understanding these errors, in particular those related to local (Hong Kong) environment. It finally took two months for all the bugs to be fixed. In the course of the trial run, it was found that even with the enhancement, FORTUNE would only take care of around 65% of user needs in Hong Kong, instead of 80% as originally contemplated. After heated discussion with members of the Hong Kong project committee, Jones insisted that the misfit was caused by some unique local require-ments of Hong Kong. "Let the systems stay where it is, only if the same problems occurred when system is tested in other locations should we consider further enhancements. Meanwhile, why don't you write some local programs to take care of these specials," he told Chan.

User Training

The user training was organized as soon as Jones arrived Hong Kong on 4 March. Participants for training included staff from Accounting, Securities Settlement and Loan Administration. Owing to some misunderstanding, FORTUNE was unable to complete the system documentation on time. In turn, standard documentation was provided but those for the enhancements were not available until several months later. Fox and Evans therefore has to hammer out some simple instruction notes. Chan assisted in modifying some of these materials as the training went along. The training went for eight weeks until late April.

Acceptance Test

After the user training, they were given hands-on trial of the new system. Incidentally, the concerns previously raised by Chan and other members of the Hong Kong project committee were again brought up by the users. Dissatisfaction was farther widespread and the New York team seemed to be fighting a lonely battle.

After several review meetings, the general manager, despite a lot of misgivings, was finally convinced that in view of the time constraints, the system had to be installed as soon as the remaining hardware peripherals arrived in mid-May.

Installation — Parallel Run

After the meeting with the project committee, Jones, Fox and Evans returned to New York and reported the status to the project steering committee. Fox also followed up with FORTUNE on the status of the system documentation. It was found that the system documentation was only 70% completed, and it would take another ten weeks before it could be accomplished. Fox argued with FORTUNE but the latter maintained that the contract only specified the delivery of the enhancement in three months' time. No mention was made to the delivery of the documentation in the contract. As the Hong Kong installation would start on 1 June, Fox mailed the incomplete version to Chan during the first week of May to prepare for the installation.

When Chan received the system documentation, he called a meeting with all the user departments to work out the plan for installation. At the same time, he engaged an analyst/programmer from a Hong Kong consultant firm, Fantastic, to work on system modification to suit the Hong Kong environment. Fantastic quoted that the modification would take three months and cost US$50,000. Chan reported this to the local committee who gave the approval using the local budget. He also told Jones about this.

On 1 June, the new FORTUNE system started to run parallel with the existing IBM RS/6000 command manual system. Because of the misfit (35%) and also that the users' procedures were not adequately changed to cope with the new environment, the operation efficiency was not improved at all. Instead, the additional reconciliation work had caused overtime pay to escalate dramatically. This was a sharp contrast to the 40% improvement in efficiency as revealed in the high-level study.

On 1 July, Chan reported the parallel run result to Jones and raised the concern over the deterioration of efficiency. Jones asked Chan to put his heart at ease and wait for the good news when the whole global system was hooked up. Jones also calmed Chan down that it would take some time for users to get used to the new system. Jones then reported to the steering committee that the parallel run in Hong Kong was a "great" success though some minor problems, primarily because of local requirements, had happened. The steering committee agreed that the production run in Hong Kong should start on 1 August 1997. Jones made no mention of the modification that was being carried out in Hong Kong.

Production Run

As instructed, Chan informed the local project committee that the production run of the program would start on 1 August. Meanwhile, the completed system documentation was received from Fox in July and copies were made to all user departments. Chan also checked with Fantastic on the progress of the enhancement and learnt that such would be available some time in September.

On 1 October, the enhanced version of FORTUNE from Fantastic was put into actual use. It was found that over 80% of the user needs was satisfied. There was around 5% saving in operation efficiency, Chan reported this to the local project committee and they all anticipated greater savings once systems of all three offices were installed and linked up. Chan also advised Jones of this who replied in a telex saying that he was delighted with the news.

Phase 4 Implementation

Chan set forth to go to Sydney for the user training and system implementation in the first week of November. In view of the right working schedule, Jones decided that the New York team would remain in New York preparing for the Phase 5 implementation while Chan would work on the Sydney implementation. If necessary, Chan could call upon additional help from New York when required. Before Chan left for Sydney, he had already worked out the training program and the installation plan with the users via telex exchanges. Along with the original enhanced version of FORTUNE, he also brought with him details of the version that Fantastic wrote for Hong Kong. In early December, the users in Sydney were given the hands-on trial of the original enhanced version. Like their Hong Kong counterpart, they were not satisfied with the program. Chan then showed them the Fantastic version and they found that, though not completely to their satisfaction, it was far better than the unmodified FORTUNE. Chan reported this to the Sydney project committee and Jones via telephone. Jones commented that this was caused by some unique requirements from the Australians, very much like Hong Kong. He said he would not object to the installation of the Fantastic version in Sydney as well. Quotation obtained from Fantastic Hone Kong was US$25,000 inclusive of travelling expenses, and the job would be completed in one month's time. Chan presented these to the Sydney committee with Jones' remarks. The general manager of Sydney approved the job using local budget.

Chan stayed on when the parallel run started in mid-December for two months. The Sydney version of the Fantastic enhancement was duly delivered to Chan in Sydney around the end of January 1998.

On 15 February 1998, Chan telexed Jones telling him that the installation in Sydney had completed; feedback from end-users was that system was "acceptable" but savings in manpower were just minimal.

Jones reported back to the steering committee that the installation was completed satisfactorily in Sydney.

Phase 5 Implementation

As early as July 1997, Fox and Evans began to develop the conversion program to convert the existing data in DATAPOINT to the IBM RS/6000 SMP. The program conversion was again contracted out to FORTUNE for the purpose of consistency. Contract terms were identical to the previous job and the cost involved was US$50,000. This was completed in September. User training on FORTUNE started on month later. When the users completed their training in November, trial runs were arranged. User's feedback was that 70% of what they were using with the existing system were met by the new FORTUNE program. The other 30% would require manual support but the job market for experienced operations staff was extremely thin. Jones enquired a quote from FORTUNE for further modifications; it would cost US$200,000.

Jones presented this to the New York project committee with the following remarks:

1. Further modifications would also benefit the other two companies in the Asia-Pacific region.
2. FORTUNE was the only supplier that could produce these modifications within the time frame. To leave the system as it was would have bad effects on operation which inevitably would impede business growth and the eventual good link-up.
3. This could never have been discovered in the high-level study and therefore should be regarded as an item under contingency.

The committee finally approved the expenses.

Jones went back to FORTUNE for the modification. This was delivered to the New York head office on Christmas Eve, 1997, but it was until mid-January when the related documentation was completed.

Parallel run of the system start in February for one month. On 1 March, Jones reported to the steering committee that result of the run, like the previous ones in Hong Kong and Sydney, was entirely fully satisfactory. The committee have the green light to start production run on 1 April 1998. This was already three months behind schedule.

On 1 May 1998, the terminals of the three offices were hooked up with modems. The general managers of the three offices all met in New York to toast to the success of the system, and also to the anticipated growth in business and profit with the new Global Risk Management System.

The Day After

Jones was later appointed Vice President to head the newly set up division on system development. Fox took up the position of the Operations Manager as the previous manager retired. Evans got the job as the Data Processing Manager of the New York office. As for Chan, he was considering an offer from another financial institution which was about to install a similar system.

On 1 July 1998, Jones was asked to present his first review report on the system to the steering committee. At the same time, the corporation's internal auditors were performing the project post-audit, and raised the question why regional expenses on modification were not included in his previous reports. Jones was expected to give his answer in his first review report. He had several sleepless nights with heaps of telexes, memos, flying in from every corner of the "globe." Some of them read as follows:

- "Urgent, could not read data transmitted from TP, 2 Apr., seemed like system error …"
- "Could not hook up to the ZZZ file of New York office. Message printed showed syntax error …"
- "Could you please respond to my memos dd 2/4, 8/4 on the problems listed regarding communication with Hong Kong and Sydney?"
- "We had sold US$10 m of ABC perpetual but suddenly realized that they were no longer in our books; we are running short position; price since went up by 10%. What's wrong with the system?"

Questions for Discussion

1. Draw an organizational chart showing the position of the project team in Worldwide Finance. Is there any weakness in the structure?
2. Construct the proposal of the project for the Capital Expenditure Committee for approval, using any available data and information mentioned in this case, together with any assumptions you may require to justify your recommendation.

3. What were the pros and cons of appointing Chan as data processing representative for both Hong Kong and Sydney offices?

4. Identify the implicit and explicit resistance from the operations staff, junior employees and branch offices appearing at any stage of the project. How did the project team respond to those resistance? What would you have done if you were the Project Manager?

5. Do you think the omission of the low-level study well-justified? What are the pros and cons for the omission?

6. Did the top management control the progress of the project team effectively? Give instances to support your answer.

7. Did Jones dominate effectively with FORTUNE, the software supplier?

8. What are the role and duties of a project manager? In your opinion, did Jones perform well?

9. What were the major causes of the three-month delay? How could that have been prevented?

10. Why was the project over-budget? How would you propose a project cost-control system?

11. What would be included in Jones's first review report? How should he tackle the identified problems the day after?

12. What contingency plans would you suggest in each phase?

15

Fashion Chain Stores Are on Their Cutting Edge

Simon S. M. Ho

The Fashion Retailing Industry

Fashion retailing business in Hong Kong had a rapid development in the last decade. More outlets are opened and the domestic market seems to still have large potential for further expansion. As living standard and consumption power become higher, consumers now are willing to spend more on clothing. Consumers also like to make comparisons; brand loyalty is lower now but they still prefer to buy well-known products.

Fashion retail outlets can be divided into three main categories. The first one is the specialty stores (e.g. Romeo Gigli, Joyce, Yves Saint Laurent, Le Saunda Yomo, etc.), which carry imported products with a few prestige brand names and aim at high-income customers. The second one is the chain store, which can be defined as "a group of retail stores essentially of the same type, franchised or centrally owned, and with some degree of centralized control of operations." Aiming at young middle-class customers, some chain store groups (like Giordano, Bossini, G-2000, Esprit, and Sparkle) even have their production bases in Hong Kong or China. Others, like Benetton and Baleno, have their products mainly imported from Europe. The third one is the independent small retailers, which usually aim at lower-income customers.

Economies of scale may be the largest motive of the rapid development of chain stores. Both expense and administrative effort can be saved by central management. Market impact is great due to the wide coverage of many outlets and in return a higher turnover. However, there is an extremely keen competition in this industry. Nearly all fashion chain store groups focus on the same market segment and provide similar products. Cut-price sales and mass media promotion methods are frequently employed. Customers will position different brands according to their own perceptions but this position changes frequently. Another problem is the relatively short product life cycle of fashions. It means that same design cannot last long; customers will quickly feel bored and seek other alternatives.

This also indicates that fashion products must be able to catch up to the market trend and that working capital should not be tied up by a large amount of inventory. Besides effective management of one's own internal operations, one major strategy used by all chain store management is to monitor customer preference and competitors' behaviours closely, and then to respond quickly to the fast-moving market. In order to achieve these purposes, access to accurate and timely information about consumers, suppliers and competitors is important. Therefore, the industry is now becoming more and more information-intensive.

The D & B Fashion Group

The rapid development of the fashion chain store industry is evidenced by the growth of D & B. D & B had only two shops in 1983 but the total number of shops now exceeds twenty-four.

D & B was founded by two owners of a local textile factory in 1982. At first, D & B focused on producing and selling premium-priced, high-quality office wear and classic knitwear. Later on, it added sport and casual wear (T-shirts, jeans, sweatshirts, cotton trousers, etc.) to its collection which was sold at lower prices. This attracted a lot of youngsters to become their regular customers. However, it did not have a set of clear strategies at that time; it just wanted to test the tastes of the public. In 1988, the number of D & B retail stores increased to fifteen. Since then, its move from a "classy" to a "popular" orientation has been very successful. D & B stands out from some other store groups through offering a whole selection of colours and styles for its fashion at a very competitive price. At the same time, it has started to put more emphasis on customer service. They provide regular sales training for all old and new sales staff, from sales assistants to shop managers.

During the year since the company was founded, the nature of its business has also shifted. Although the firm still produces fashions by its manufacturing division, its primary business is as a fashion retailer. D & B's own factory produces only 30% of the stock it sells. It purchases the remaining 70% from several local manufacturers with the D & B labels put on the products. With its own, though small, manufacturing facilities, urgent orders can be delivered to the outlets within three weeks after placing an order. Also, D & B's factory can produce small quantity of trial products. Products which become popular can then be mass produced by other suppliers.

D & B is ambitious to become a competitive participant in the industry. Annual real sales growth rate of over 80% was realized for most of the years until three years ago. Two years ago, D & B increased its retail stores to twenty, and the business turnover was over HK$85 million. However, it continues to have to face very keen and intense competition. For instance, four years ago, there was only one representative competitor near D & B's Mong Kok outlet, but by last year there were four. In particular, staff at D & B were surprised to discover that one of D & B's competitors, Giordano, was expanding their chain of outlets much more rapidly and had five retail stores set up just in central Mong Kok.

Sales and profits for D & B had grown at a steady rate until the last two years, even with the addition of two new stores in last year. D & B has failed to meet forecasts in the last two years and has performed at a slower rate than several major competitors. Management at D & B believes this was mainly due to intensified competition in the industry. Nevertheless, senior executives at D & B know that overall fashion consumption in Hong Kong is still growing (see Figures 1–3), although they are not certain to what extent the trend will continue.

Currently, a mini-computer and a cluster of microcomputers are used in the head office primarily in the following application areas:

- Payroll
- Inventory control (merchandise)

Figure 1: Statistics for Retail Trades in Clothing and Allied Products, 1988–1993

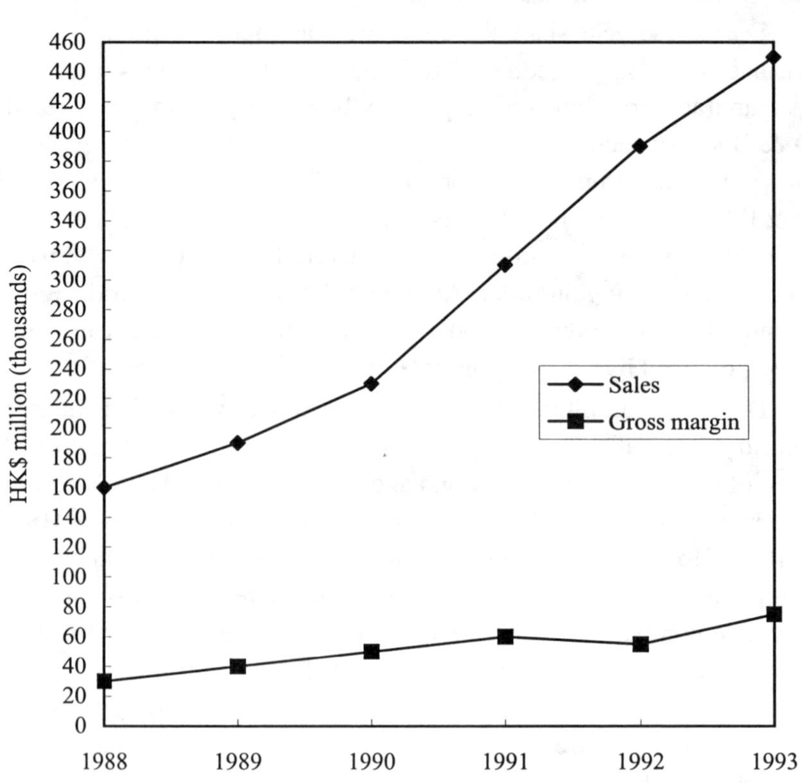

Source: *Hong Kong Annual Digest of Statistics* (Hong Kong Government: Census and Statistics Department, 1995).

- General accounting
- Sales analysis

About one-fourth of the outlet shops, on an experimental basis, have installed a stand-alone microcomputer to generate invoices and sales transaction lists. However, these computers have no linking with the head office's systems or other stores' microcomputers. For most shops,

Figure 2: Index of Retail Sales in Clothing & Allied Products, 1988–1995

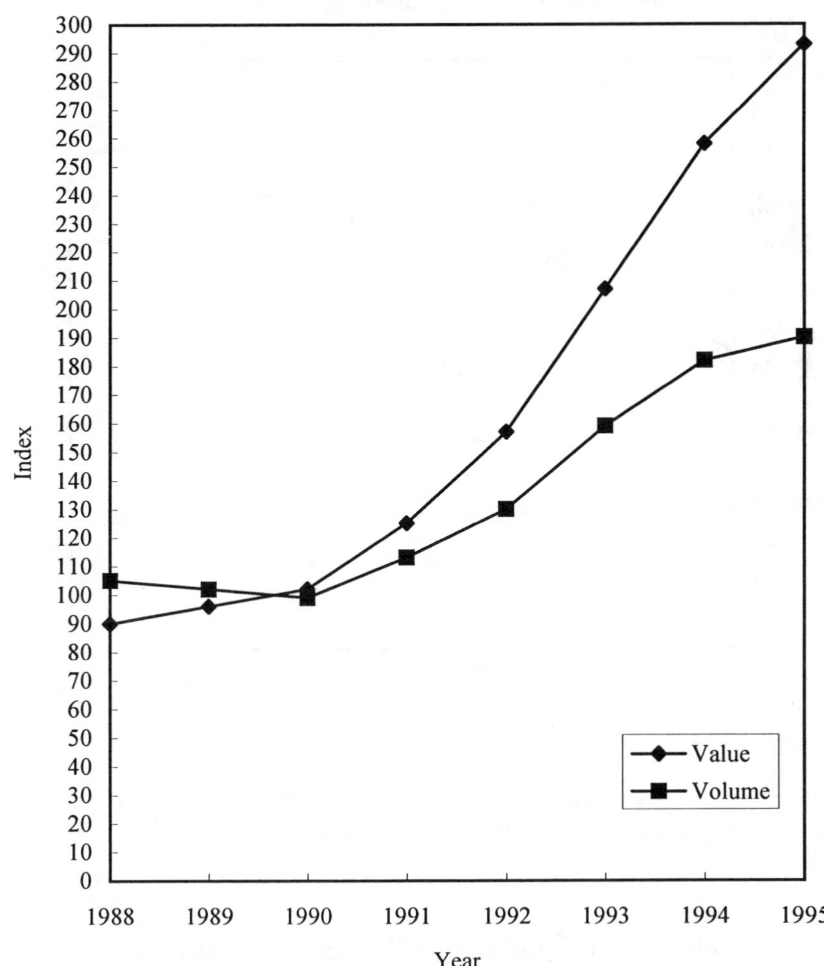

Source: *Hong Kong Monthly Digest of Statistics* (Hong Kong Government: Census and Statistics Department, March 1995).

sales transactions by customers are still written up by salespersons. Sales slips are sent weekly to the Electronic Data Processing (EDP) department. The sorted sales transaction data are then used to update the stock and sales master files. Corporate and store managers also depend

**Figure 3: Consumption Expenditure of Clothing and Allied Products at
Constant Prices (1990) and Market Prices (1986)**

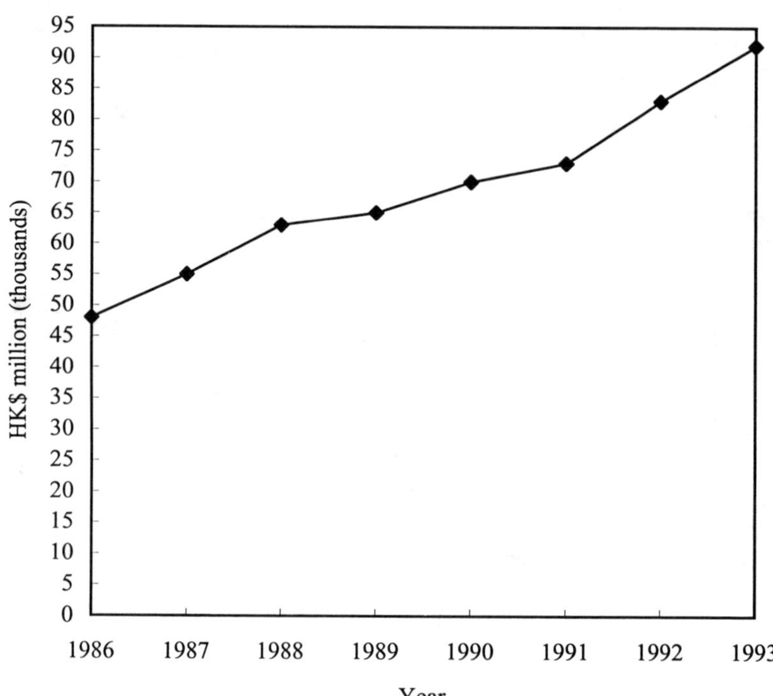

Source: *Estimates of Gross Domestic Products 1961 to 1994* (Hong Kong
Government: Census and Statistics Department, March 1995).

on the weekly sales analysis reports that tell them the trends in sales
performance of various products.

The Chairman's Encounters

Being a high-school graduate, Charles Cha, aged 44, the co-founder and
Executive Director of D & B, gained his experience and "lessons" from
working in garment factories. Cha has over thirty years' experience of
fashion manufacturing and merchandising. Although he is skilled in
raising capital and he has accumulated enough funds to get the company

going and expanding, he is also keen on cost control. With his enthusiasm in the business and adequate financial resources, the company grew in size from two stores to twenty-four stores now.

Cha devoted much of his time to the management of D & B, although he is also holding several other business. He has regular meetings with all the department heads and senior store managers every month to discuss all sort of matters. He also makes visits to the shops occasionally in order to understand the business better and to encourage the sales staff there. He said that it would build company morale by showing that the Chairman cares about the employees. In fact, most of the employees feel satisfied with the working conditions and fringe benefits offered by their company.

During a recent visit in the Tsim Sha Tsui East branch, he noticed that salespersons were just too busy in writing up sales slips or running around to check stock availability. Customers on the sales floor seemed to think that they did not receive adequate prompt service and personal attention. He head the following comments from the customer:

- "Hey! Jeff, you see! How stupid the cashier is! Even with the help of the microcomputer, she still proceeds dead slowly!"
- "How come I have to wait for such a long time? I have already waited for over ten minutes to charge out with my credit card?"
- "I don't understand why I have to wait for ten minutes to know that the shop does not carry the colour I want."

Because Cha had seldom heard such expressions from the customers during his past visits, he therefore put the blame on the retail branch manager. However, the branch manager claimed that there were long queues in other branches too because some of the cashiers were newly employed and it was during the sale period. Cha was dissatisfied with the explanation and so he decided to include this issue in the next business meeting.

Cha had made visits to five other shops in different districts. He went into the storerooms of all these shops. Faced with the hills of clothing products, he thought, "Something really must be done here." In all the five shops he visited, Cha also found that they all had a "crazy sale" counter for short-sleeve shirts. The price was nearly half of the original. "It's still Summer. Why do they cut the price so early?" Cha thought. When he came back to the head office, he asked Marcus Mak, the Director of Marketing and Sales.

Cha: Marcus, why are there big sales on short-sleeve shirts even it is still Summer?

Mak: You probably have recognized, Mr. Cha, that youngsters today tend to wear long-sleeve shirts rather than short sleeves. Last year, long-sleeve shirts of our company constituted 25% of our total revenues. Therefore we'd like to clear the short-sleeve stock as soon as possible and therefore a "crazy sale" counter is set up in nearly every store.

The Top Executive Meeting

On one Monday morning in August, several senior executives (including Marcus Mak, the Director of Marketing and Sales; Francis Fan, the Director of Finance; and Peter Pau, the EDP Manager) and two senior store managers (Steve Shum and Alice Au) met in Cha's "tai-ban" office. In fact, such a meeting has been expected for weeks. Eventually it came. Cha began to talk.

Cha: Good morning folks. Let's go straight to business. As you probably saw from the most recent sales report, they don't look good. Our sales figure has only increased by 28% in the past six months. Considering that we aimed at increasing our turnover for 65% this year, I wonder if we can achieve this. I just don't understand why this happens as I know that overall clothing consumption in Hong Kong is growing. I'd like to hear your ideas. Marcus, why don't you start first?

Mak: I realize that, Mr. Cha. Well, we just haven't had the marketing budget to do the things we should have done. We have already done everything that should be done with the amount of money allocated to us. Two of our staff members keep carrying out small-scale market surveys of consumers' tastes regularly. Traditional product testing is also carried out at the end of each season. We have to give "this thing" extra sales force and time. On the other hand, the budgets for promoting and advertising are certainly not sufficient. I've told you that all along. Our competitor has sunk millions into advertising. If more funds can be allocated to the promotion campaigns, I am quite sure that our sales will increase, and the company's image will also be upgraded as well.

Cha: We certainly need to know where the customers are and what type of products they want to buy, but I don't know to what extent it helps by hiring three or four new market researchers to get this information. Francis, what are your thoughts on the sales performance and the advertising budget?

Fan: I doubt if we can boost up the figures substantially with more advertising. The present advertising expenditure has already taken up about 10% of the total company expenses. I think Mak you should have a tighter control over the financial resources instead. In fact, the cost of operations, such as wages, rents, and raw materials, has increased substantially in the past year. I feel that D & B could provide fewer choices using more classic designs presented in a modern and attractive format. Products with such design are relatively unaffected by fashion cycles and can achieve further economy of scale.

Cha: This seems rather tricky, and obviously we need to re-evaluate our strategic plan for our products and marketing from time to time.

Fan: There is one thing which I'd like to mention. As you may know, one of our major product suppliers always delays our orders, and, because of this, we missed several peak sales periods. That does contribute a great loss of sales. Furthermore, since our demands fluctuate and there are no fixed contracts, one or two suppliers have once sold the available capacity to other sources and ended up with problems with us. The paper communication delays often worsen the ordering, shipping and payment tasks.

Cha: That's really a problem. Lack of sufficient control of our product supplies would certainly hamper the competitiveness of

	our business. Em.… How about trying to switch to some other suppliers in the short run?
Mak:	I do not agree to that, Mr. Cha. Since we have not much contact with other manufacturers, I am not sure whether they can meet our requirements or not. And up to now, we have maintained quite a good relationship with our current suppliers. They are familiar with our product requirements. So it is not a good idea to shift to other manufacturers.
Fan:	Maybe we can turn to one or two other manufacturers on a few products for three months as a test. If the lead time is significantly reduced, we shall place most of the orders with them. I think we've got no other choice.

(There was then a deep silence.)

Cha:	There are also other things on which I would like to hear your thinking. I visited several branches two weeks ago. I have noticed that the customers have to wait for a long time to pay, and sometimes it takes ten minutes to find out that the specific size or colour that a customer wants is not available. I think this does affect our image and business. I just wonder why this happens. What do you think about the problem, Alice?
Au:	One thing I have in mind is that the computer stock list prepared by the head office is always outdated and contains errors from time to time. It is probably due to the remoteness of our location and the poor implementation of the computer system. So, we rely on our outlet staff to maintain the stock list. Recently, I found it too difficult to do this by hand accurately. We have been too busy in serving the customers. However, we are losing sales because we cannot get updated information on product availability.
Cha:	Yes, I heard about the problem from other outlets as well. Initially, we had only a few product items. But now we offer so many different kinds of items with different styles and colours. As we open more chain stores, it seems to me that the problem is becoming more serious. What do you think, Steve?
Shum:	I think this problem can be resolved by allocating more sales manpower for each store. We may also ask one salesgirl to help

the store manager to sum up the amount in the invoices each day and update the stock list.

Cha: I don't think that is a very good alternative as the salespersons should spend their time concentrating on customer services on the sales floor. Instead, I think one way to reverse the sales trend may be to give more prompt service and personal attention to the customers.

Shum: Another matter I would like to mention is that, during peak season (e.g. on-sale or X'mas period and some special occasions), there will be unexpected increases in demand. Although the store can send orders to the central office to request for more stock, it requires at least two days for the stock to be delivered from the central warehouse. I think this is a problem that deserves attention.

Cha: By the way, I am thinking of minimizing the stock-out chances in each store by transferring some inventories among its near-by outlets when needed. One shop can request the required stock from other nearby D & B stores if they have it. I think stock transfer can lower the stock level and reduce the possibility of stock-out.

Au: It sounds ideal but this will make our inventory system even more complicated. We just don't have the manpower to keep track of stock. There will also be additional communication and paperwork for inter-outlet transfers.

Cha: Marcus, do you have other points you want to raise?

Mak: We all understand that, in order to cope better with the keen competition, instant and accurate information has to be collected about the popular style, size, colour, price, quality and customer segment for decision making. But currently our managers have to depend on weekly sales analysis reports that all use the same report format. I appreciate how much the existing systems have already brought to us. But I understand that our competitors are already figuring out some new sales automation and information systems which enable them to avoid keeping large amount of stocks and have immediate responses to the ongoing market. They are also using new computer systems to analyse the advertising budget and maximize selling space.

Pau: I've heard about that of course. We are always looking for more funds for developing new applications and employing more people to satisfy your guys' demands. But cost justification for many new systems ideas is not that easy. There are also other problems concerning operational and behavioural feasibility.

Au: I believe using sales automation systems in each store would significantly reduce the time needed by a salesperson to complete a sale transaction. This would not only improve customer service, but also free salespersons to serve more customers.

Fan: I have reservations on what you said, Alice. Sales automation would involve a large initial investment and resistance to the technology by some salespersons and managers. I fear that there will be a loss of salespersons and customer interactions. Too much automation may also cause our managers become too dependent on computers. I believe there are other better solutions to solve our current problems.

Cha: Since fashion has a very short product life cycle, "quick response" is a must in this market. We must not let our working capital be tied up by a large inventory. This will tighten our cash flow and the company will suffer considerably. Our company is making a profit, and we can get financing when we know ahead of time that we need it. If we cannot remove the defects of the present operations, we have to postpone our expansion plan, and our market share will be eroded away. But of course, any solution to our current problems must be feasible and cost-justified. Paul and Marcus, you'd better start making a study of the status of our operations and systems, and give a proposal as soon as possible. We may hire an outside consultant to help us if necessary.

Pau and Marcus nodded reluctantly. Cha tried to make a final remark.

Cha: Since I have to go in a couple of minutes, would you all please study those issues and discuss with me your concrete plan in the next meeting? I'm sure we'll find a solution.

Cha grimaced as he left his office. And this concluded the meeting.

Questions for Discussion

1. Analyse the fashion retailing industry (with D & B as one of the competitors) with regard to the industry's competition and critical success factors.
2. From a systems standpoint, identify and discuss the major problem(s) that D & B is experiencing. What are symptoms of the problem(s)?
3. Applying McFarlan-McKenny's strategic grid for information systems planning, which quadrant is D & B currently in? Which quadrant should it move to? What information management approach strategy should D & B adopt in the long run?
4. Using Michael Porter's "value chain" model, what activities can be included in the value chain for D & B? Explain and give examples of how information technology (IT) and information systems (IS) can be used to support these activities.
5. Using Michael Porter's "competitive forces" and "competitive strategy" models, explain (and give examples if appropriate) how IT/IS can:
   - affect competition in the fashion retail industry?
   - be used as a competitive weapon and increase D & B's competitive advantage?
   - spawn whole new business opportunities in the fashion industry or in another related industry?
6. In view of D & B's case situation, identify and evaluate several alternative solutions. Justify the best course of action selected. Explain any assumptions you made in completing your analysis.

References

Benjamin, I., J. F. Rockart, Michael S. Scott Morton, and John Wyman. "Information Technology: A Strategic Opportunity." *Sloan Management Review* (Spring 1984), pp. 3–4.

Cash, J. and B. Konsynaski. "Information Systems Redraws Competitive Boundaries." *Harvard Business Review* (March–April 1985), pp. 134–42.

Earl, M. E. "The New and the Old of Business Process Redesign." *Journal of Strategic Information Systems*, No. 3 (1994), pp. 5–22.

Ives, B. and G. P. Learmouth. "The Information System as a Competitive Weapon." *Communication of the ACM* (December 1984), pp. 1193.

McFarlan, F. W. "Information Technology Changes the Way You Compete." *Harvard Business Review* (May–June 1984), pp. 98–103.

McFarlan, F. W. and J. L. McKenny. *Corporate Information Systems*. Homewood, Ill.: Richard D. Irwin, 1983, pp. 14–16.

Porter, M. E. "How Competitive Forces Shape Strategy." *Harvard Business Review* (March–April 1979), pp. 137–45.

Porter, M. E. and V. E. Millar. "How Information Gives You Competitive Advantage." *Harvard Business Review* (July–August 1985), pp. 149–61.

Russell, J. H. and M. Vitale. "Creating Competitive Advantage with Interorganisation Systems." *MIS Quarterly* (June 1988), pp. 153–56.

Venkatraman, N. "IT-enabled Business Transformation: From Automation to Business Scope Redefinition." *Sloan Management Review* (Winter 1994), pp. 73–87.

Wiseman, C. *Strategic Information Systems*. Homewood, Ill.: Richard D. Irwin, 1988.

Strategic Information Systems Planning at Cathay Pacific Airways

Shao Yuanpu and Liao Shaoyi

Introduction

Strategic information systems planning begins with the business, its future and its competitiveness. This case study deals with a situation analysis of its use of information systems. Specifically, it outlines the business, business strategies and competition. This is followed by a detailed study on each system's contribution to the business (its heavy use to support operational activities). The case study concludes with a few intriguing questions to explore further on strategic information systems planning.

Company Background

Cathay Pacific Airways Limited (CPA) was established in 1946. It is a subsidiary company of the Swire Group and is a public company listed in the Hong Kong Stock Exchange and the London Stock Exchange. The company first started a charter operation flying cargoes between Asia and Australia.

CPA has enjoyed a rapid growth in the past fifty years. By the end of 1995, it was providing scheduled passenger and cargo services to forty-six cities in twenty-seven countries and territories with 14,744 employees around the world. In addition to flight services, CPA also provides other aviation-related services such as catering, aircraft overhaul and maintenance, airport security, cargo handling and computerized reservation system through its subsidiary and associated companies.

Business Strategy

Three major business strategies were identified in the company's operation.

Importance of Asia Market

In order to maintain its market share, the company's business focuses on short haul routes with emphasis on Northeast Asia in developing, delivering and promoting successful Asian products. Moreover, the company values the market in China and plans to capitalize on its position in the market. However, the emphasis on the strategies for the route planning in Northeast Asia does not reflect that the company is going to give up the global market. The company still maintains and selectively adds long haul routes with appropriate products.

Cost Awareness

Another business strategy is to reduce the cost so that it could meet the desired profitability margin. Several measures were identified by the management:

- Capitalizing on the existing capacity.
- Pursuing an aggressive cost management.
- Improving the revenue management.
- Employing a tighter management of investments (for cost reduction).
- Investing and managing airline-related business (with control).

Securing New Business Opportunities

The company has been actively identifying new business opportunities for development. The move to invest in Chek Lap Kok, Hong Kong's new airport, is part of a wide range of its investments in the future and will be the biggest event in its fifty-year history. The company will be investing in the operational and support facilities at Chek Lap Kok. The inauguration of Chek Lap Kok will open up many new commercial, business and marketing opportunities for the company. Meanwhile, the investments cover radical new applications for information technology.

Competition

Asian skies are still the fast-growing and potentially the richest market in the world. It has been estimated that Asia, accounting for 30% of world air travel, would generate 50% of business within a decade. Asian airlines have met other international players' challenges. Profit margin has decreased in recent years. Asian airlines have started cost-cutting exercises and many of these airlines complain about the unfair competition from airlines based outside Asia, notably the American airlines.

The Current Use of Information Systems

The main focus of this section is to evaluate the application areas of information systems in the company. The scale of the existing application platforms used in the company ranges from mainframe to stand alone personal computers (PCs). Owing to the historical background (i.e. mainframe dominated the computer industry at that time), many on-line applications were developed by using mainframe as the major platform. For the customer services system, it used the Unisys Mainframe OS/1100 series machine that has been mainly used to run FORTRAN-written applications. For the corporate system, it used IBM Mainframe ES9000 that has been used to run DB2, ADABAS and Natural-written applications. It provided superior processing power over 1980s.

With the popularity of PC in recent decade, the company began to make use of this equipment. Apart from using for the word-processing purpose, some small applications were developed on PC that has been connected through the local area network (LAN). At the same time, a link between the mainframe and the PCs has been built up so that it is more user-friendly and convenient to use the PC's attractive interface, such as the OS/2 interface to access the mainframe database. Moreover,

Table 1: Major Applications Used by the Company

Applications name	Description	Hardware				Customer orientation				Business functions supportiveness			
		Unisys	IBM	PC	Unix	H	M	L	Nil	H	M	L	Nil
TOURS	Tour product automation	*					*			*			
CUPID	Reservation and distribution system	*	*			*				*			
CUPAC	Passenger acceptance and department system	*				*				*			
ABC	Boarding control system			*				*				*	
CRMS	Customer relations system		*					*			*		
CUDOS	Customer and prospect system		*	*			*			*			
CAPITAL	Integrated ticket A/C link system		*				*						*
RAS	Revenue analysis system		*					*					*
REFLEX	Inflight survey		*					*				*	
BIDT	Billing information data tapes		*				*				*		
CLUBS PC	MP Club PC system			*				*				*	
COMS PC	Outport marketing system			*				*			*		
HandHeld	MPO check-in			*				*				*	
PAB	Price activity book		*				*				*		

Table 1: (Cont'd)

Applications name	Description	Hardware				Customer orientation				Business functions supportiveness			
		Unisys	IBM	PC	Unix	H	M	L	Nil	H	M	L	Nil
REVTAB	Revenue table		*						*				*
PASSAGES	FTP access system	*							*			*	
CRESTA	Revenue estimation system		*						*			*	
OPFM	Outport forecasting models			*					*				*
CUBIC	Cargo booking system	*				*				*			
MCS	Aircraft movement control				*			*		*			
ICRS	Crew rostering				*				*		*		
RAS/PC	Revenue analysis system for outport			*					*			*	
SMKIT	Sales manager's kit		*	*					*		*		
YDC	Young discovers' club		*				*					*	
POOL	Pool statistics system		*						*				*
PAXPR2	Auto ticket system		*				*				*		
PROS	Passenger revenue optimization system			*			*					*	
QIKCHK	Quick check-in			*			*					*	
QIKRES	Quick reservation			*				*			*		

Notes: (1) H = High; M = Medium; L = Low.
      (2) Unisys/IBM are mainframe system.

the company has started stepping in the Unix world which offers high processing power and easier adoption of application software from outside suppliers.

Table 1 summarizes the major types of applications used in the company. The classification is based on the three main types of hardware used, the customer orientation and the business functions supportiveness.

Evaluation of the Current Use of Information Systems

High Mainframe Usage

From the above application list, there are 19 out of 29 applications (i.e. around 65%) running under the mainframe platform. Table 1 also shows that over 70% of these applications are run on IBM mainframe. Thus, these statistics reflect that the company attaches the importance to the use of IBM mainframe instead of other mainframes.

However, if the company relies solely on the use of single mainframe system platform, there may come out another problem that affects the strategic use of information technology (IT) and information systems (IS). Simply speaking, the bargaining power will be weakened if Porter's theory of competitive advantage is applied. In addition, it may prohibit the development or the use of certain information systems. This can be supported by the use of the new technology such as the client/server, which is different from the concept used in the mainframe system.

Business Function-based Applications

The main objectives of information systems are to support the business and to deliver the right information at the right time. From Table 1, there are 24 out of 29 applications that support the business functions in different levels. These business functions range from external processes, such as reservation on flights and other airlines, to internal processes, such as revenue forecasting and billing reconciliation.

Transactions-based Applications

The main tasks of these applications are to meet operational needs. If we look at the relationship between applications and customer-related objectives, these applications mainly satisfy the needs of those operational staff in lower levels. For instance, the reservation system called "CUPID" is a very successful application in the company. However, the main objectives of this system are to:

- Record the customer booking timely and accurately.
- Allow easy access to Cathay Pacific product for the customers.
- Advance the procedures of the seat reservation.

End-user Computing

With the proliferation of PCs and increasing demand to process information, the end-user computing environment has been advocated in many organizations. This trend has become one of the most important in IS field. The company has deployed a mainframe-based end-user computing platform which offers statistical analysis, ranging from passenger information, commercial inflight stock information, accounting information to staff information.

Conclusion

This case study analysed the company's business and its current use of information technology in terms of IT contribution to the business. The analysis implies that the information systems developed in the company are essential to current operations and their management, but are not at the heart of the company's strategic development. Strategic information systems are those that provide competitive advantages to the company over others.

Questions for Discussion

1. How does people approach the strategic planning of new information systems?

2. Following the current IS appraisal in the company, can you suggest some types of strategic information systems? Please argue for what you suggest.
3. How do you evaluate the competitive role of information systems in the airline industry?

Acknowledgements

The authors wish to thank Peter Ng for research assistance.

Class Adoption

We shall provide a free inspection copy to each teaching professional who is interested in reviewing our titles in this series for adoption in his courses. Supplementary materials, such as Teaching Notes, will also be provided free if the titles have been adopted. However, The Chinese University Press reserves the right to refuse request for complimentary copies which are not within its complimentary copy policy.

For inspection copies, please write using your institution's letterhead indicating your class size and the intended adoption date to:

Business Manager
The Chinese University Press
The Chinese University of Hong Kong
Sha Tin
New Territories
Hong Kong
Telephone: (852) 2609 6508 / 2609 6500
Facsimile: (852) 2603 6692

MANAGEMENT DEVELOPMENT SERIES

Forthcoming

Hong Kong Management Cases for Supervisors

Hong Kong Management Cases in Human Resources Management

Already published

Hong Kong Management Cases in Hotel Management

Hong Kong Management Cases in Marketing

專業管理叢書

即將出版

《管理人經濟學》

《管理學原理》

已刊書目

《香港商業法》

《組織行爲與人事管理》

《管理資訊系統》

《數量方法的管理應用》

Annual Case Writing Competition

Write to Win

Since 1988, The Management Development Centre of Hong Kong has started organizing the Annual Case Writer of the Year Competitions. With the sponsorship of the American Chamber of Commerce Charitable Foundation, the competitions have been most successful and attracted a large number of good quality case submission every year.

For further information about the Case Writing Competition, please call or write to the Executive Officer of The Management Development Centre of Hong Kong at 11/F., VTC Tower, 27 Wood Road, Wan Chai, Hong Kong (Tel: 2836 1816, Fax: 2572 7130).

The Case Study Group of Hong Kong

The Case Study Group of Hong Kong was formed in 1987 with the objective of promoting case method for management teaching and training in the territory. With administrative and advisory support from The Management Development Centre of Hong Kong, the Group has regular meetings and seminars during which cases are presented.

The Case Study Group is open to those in Hong Kong who are involved in the use of case materials and methods in management training and development (whether by occupation or interest).

If you will complete the details below, we will add your name to our mailing list and notify you of all forthcoming activities.

Name (Last, First):	
HKID No.:	
Job Title:	
Company Name:	
Company Address:	
Home Address:	
Telephone (office):	
Fax (office):	
Specialized area:	

Please return to:
Ms. May Li
The Management Development Centre of Hong Kong,
11/F., VTC Tower, 27 Wood Road, Wan Chai,
Hong Kong

Tel : 2836 1818
Fax : 2572 7130